The Religion of Irish Dissent, 1650–1800

In the same series:

The Irish Dissenting Tradition, 1650–1750

The Religion of
Irish Dissent
1650–1800

EDITED BY

Kevin Herlihy

FOUR COURTS PRESS

Set in 10.5 on 12.5 point Ehrhardt for
FOUR COURTS PRESS LTD
Kill Lane, Blackrock, Co. Dublin, Ireland
and in North America
FOUR COURTS PRESS LTD
c/o ISBS, 5804 NE Hassalo Street, Portland, OR 97213.

A catalogue record for this title
is available from the British Library.

ISBN 1-85182-236-4

This book was printed on a wood-free
and an acid-free paper.

Printed in Great Britain
by Antony Rowe Ltd, Chippenham, Wilts.

Contents

Preface

This book is a volume of proceedings from an annual conference on Irish Dissent which was held at Marsh's Library, Dublin on 18 March 1995. Although this book is about religion it is not intended to be an exhaustive study of that subject. Because the conference was for one day only certain aspects of religion have been examined by the contributors. Using the terminolgy of Professor Patrick Collinson the work contained in the chapters contains both the 'vertical' and the 'horizontal' historical perspectives. The 'vertical' interest is present because of the relationship of the writers to the subject, but the strength of that relationship varies from writer to writer. The 'horizontal' aspect is also clearly present in that the theme of religion is placed by the authors within the wider context of early modern Irish society

The volume is divided into three parts. In part one larger issues concerning religion are considered. In the first chapter Alan Ford explores the religious framework of early seventeenth-century Irish Protestants to descry the 'proto-history' of one type of religious dissent in Ireland. The capacious character of the established church at that time apportioned latitude enough that alienation and marginalisation did not occur in any significant segments of the Irish Protestant community. Alongside a number of significant theological differences in the Protestant community was the flexibility of the incumbents. In the second chapter Raymond Gillespie investigates and describes the personal experience of prayer in late seventeenth-century Ireland. Prayer was an act of devotion that formed an indispensable part of the heart of nonconformist religious experience. Because nonconformist religion placed great emphasis on personal experience, prayer, both public and private, was a most important type of experience because it was considered to be part of personal revelation. Furthermore, prayer was a particularly meaningful source of authority for devising distinctive ecclesiastical institutions.

In part two particular aspects of religion in various dissenting societies are considered. In the first paper an explanation is given to account for the metamorphose of Irish Baptist piety which moved from boldness and optimism to misgiving and apprehension. In the following essay Richard S. Harrison charts the changing attitudes and developments of Irish Quaker spirituality. Quakers, like the Baptists, had to make adjustments in their otherworldly considerations due to changing circumstances, both inside and outside their community, which entailed compromise. This exposition plots the course that the Irish Quaker leadership took. Raymond Hylton provides an outline of Huguenot progress, or lack of progress, in Ireland, along with a description and analysis of particular Huguenot religious practices. Professor Finlay Holmes concludes this section by demonstrating, with some wit, the popular reaction of Presbyterian constituents to efforts at religious innovation instigated by an educated elite, which was made up of both the laity and the ministry, in early eighteenth-century Ulster.

In the final part a document relevant to this study, *The Narrative of the Case of Miles Crowly*, has been reproduced and preceded by an elucidation, rather than a complete commentary, of the text. There are some serious exigetical problems due to the motives of the author. Nevertheless, their is much to be gleaned, although skeptically, from pamphlets of this type. The tract is enlightening in relation to differences in religious attitudes that existed in late eighteenth-century Ireland. In addition, the religious ideas that separated Catholics and Protestants, as well as nonconformists and the established church, in the later half of the eighteenth century are discernable in the text in spite of the disingenuous attitude of the author.

* * *

I would like to recognise the following people and institutions for the help they have provided. First and foremost thanks are due to Trinity College, Dublin for a wide variety of assistance in making the conference a success and the publication of this book possible. I am very grateful to the Department of Modern History and especially Professor Aidan Clarke for support in this project, chairing papers and valuable guidance; Muriel McCarthy for the splendid hospitality and warm atmosphere at Marsh's Library; the Ancient & Benevolent Order of the Friendly Brothers of St Patrick for providing the wonderful venue for the conference dinner and most of all to the contributors for the effort that they exerted and to those that showed their interest by attending the presentations.

KEVIN HERLIHY

The Origins of Irish Dissent

ALAN FORD

'The origins of dissent' is in many respects an old fashioned title, redolent of the innumerable articles in Victorian journals with titles like 'Pioneers of Congregationalism'. Such scholarship is readily classifiable: it represents what has been labelled 'vertical history'—the history of a particular church, usually written by an 'insider' 'which has been all about origins, title-deeds, pedigree and descent'.[1] It is a notable feature of those religious traditions that dissented from the established church, since defining and tracing the origins of their distinctiveness and difference from the establishment was an essential part of their self-image. And indeed, this attempt to sort out the roots of Irish dissent, exhuming the names of obscure sectarians who briefly settled in remote places in Ireland in the period after the Reformation, will have a whiff of that Victorian style of history.

But I also have three wider, more 'modern' aims. First, I wish to take a slightly perverse chronological perspective, looking not at the obvious ferment, political and religious, of the 1640s and 1650s which, I readily accept, gave birth to Irish nonconformity, but an unfashionably early period in the history of Irish dissent, the later sixteenth and early seventeenth centuries, and the settlement of religion under Elizabeth and the opposition it aroused, prior to the Irish rebellion in 1641—what might be termed the pre-history of Irish dissent. Second, I want to place these developments in the context not just of Ireland, but of the three kingdoms and their interaction with Ireland. And finally, I want to place the origins of Irish dissent not within the pious confines of the vertical history of each sect, but in the horizontal setting of post-reformation piety and religion.

I

To begin with the broader geographical context. No one would argue that the Irish Protestant religion was home-grown. The primacy of the English model

---

1 Patrick Collinson, 'The vertical and the horizontal in religious history: internal and external integration of the subject', in Alan Ford, James McGuire and Kenneth Milne (eds), *As by Law Established. The Church of Ireland Since the Reformation* (Dublin, 1995), p. 18; see also Patrick Collinson, 'Towards a broader understanding of the early dissenter tradition', in idem, *Godly People. Essays on English Protestantism and Puritanism* (London, 1983).

hardly needs stressing: the Reformation was an English import, and to a large extent remained such for much of its early history in Ireland. The Irish Acts of Uniformity and Supremacy of 1560 were based upon, indeed copied from is more accurate, the Elizabethan legislation in England. And not only the definition of Protestant establishment, but dissent from it, was, as Miller has observed of the nineteenth century, closely linked to the process of immigration across the Irish sea, each sect focusing its efforts on distinct colonial communities.[2] The 'pre-history' of dissent in England, is, as a result, of primary importance in identifying the sources for dissent in late sixteenth century and early seventeenth century Ireland.[3]

Two groups, one tiny, one much larger, can be identified as the ancestors of the later dissenting tradition in England: the Separatists and the Puritans. The roots of English separatism can be traced back to the Marian martyrs and followed through the later sixteenth century as they reject the Elizabethan settlement. Separatists' defining characteristics were, of course, a rejection of the all encompassing national Church of England, with all its compromises and contradictions, and a consequent determination to create purer congregations based upon believers and firm biblical principles. The Puritan movement can similarly be dated to the early years of Elizabeth's reign, though it remained, by and large, within the confines of the established church, and, apart from those 'hasty' members who chose to separate, continued to advocate a national church. The attempt by English Puritans to create Presbyterian structures within the Church of England ended in defeat in the late 1580s. Subsequently English Puritans were less concerned with church government than with the creation of godly communities at a parochial level, often with the enthusiastic support of like-minded gentry or civic leaders.[4]

The translation of English dissent across the Irish sea can be illustrated with apparent straightforwardness by tracing how individual English dissenters settled in Ireland. The process of exporting English dissent began soon after the Elizabethan settlement, as Puritan ministers, forced out of England, sought refuge in Ireland. The collapse of the English Presbyterian movement saw another influx after 1590, as distinguished English academics and preachers such as Walter Travers, Humphrey Fenn and Henry Alvey, sought to reconstruct their shattered careers in Ireland. Trinity College Dublin, safely tucked away from the gaze of the authorities in England, attracted a number of Puritan students from England. The extensive movement of settlers from

2 D.W. Miller, 'Presbyterianism and "modernization" in Ulster' in *Past & Present*, lxxx (1978), p. 73.

3 For the concept of pre-history see B.R. White, *The English Separatist Tradition: from the Marian Martyrs to the Pilgrim Fathers* (Oxford, 1971), p. xii; Collinson, 'Early Dissenter Tradition', pp. 527f.

4 Patrick Collinson, *The Elizabethan Puritan Movement* (London, 1967); P.G. Lake, *Moderate Puritans and the Elizabethan Church* (Cambridge, 1982).

England to Ireland in the late sixteenth and early seventeenth centuries further facilitated the export not merely of Puritan clergy, but also of a number of godly gentry.[5]

English Separatists likewise sought refuge in Ireland, especially after the legislation against sectaries and the execution of John Penry and Henry Barrow in 1593. Meredith Hanmer, chancellor of Ossory and noted historian, when listing nonconformist activity in Dublin in the late 1590s distinguished between Puritans and sectaries, and preserved a hostile list of Separatist beliefs.[6] In 1594 an unnamed Separatist in Ireland rejected the established church 'its public worship, and its ministers, bishops, archbishops', declaring that it was 'in bondage and beareth the yoke of antichrist'.[7] It is possible that the anonymous Separatist writer might have been Henry Ainsworth, who, in the early 1590s came to Ireland before moving on to the Netherlands where he was to play such an important role in the exile English congregation.[8] Here too, colonisation provided opportunities for dissenters. In 1598, a commentator on the Munster plantation complained at the lack of control over the religious outlook of the Munster planters, which had resulted in 'Papists, Puritans, Brownists, atheists' settling in the province.[9] A further attempt to found a Separatist community in Ireland came in the early 1620s, when a London dissenting minister, with his congregation, settled in Carrickfergus, County Antrim. When he died some two years later, however, they returned to England.[10] Another party of Separatists from London settled in Antrim in the early 1630s.[11] There is even mention of an English Anabaptist finding refuge in Ireland.[12]

5 For a detailed treatment of English Puritanism in Ireland, see Alan Ford, 'The Church of Ireland, 1558–1634: a Puritan Church?', in Alan Ford, James McGuire and Kenneth Milne (eds), *As by Law Established. The Church of Ireland since the Reformation* (Dublin, 1995), pp. 52–68.

6 SP 63/214/36, fols 214r, 216r.

7 Henry Barrow, *Mr H. Barrows Platform. Which may Serve as a Preparation to Purge away Prelatism* ([London], [1611]), sig. [C6v].

8 D.N.B., s.v. Henry Ainsworth; H.M. Dexter, *The Congregationalism of the Last Three Hundred Years, as seen in its Literature* (New York, 1880), pp. 270, 364; Champlin Burrage, *The early English Dissenters in the Light of Recent Research (1550–1641)* (2 vols., Cambridge, 1912), i, 187; White, *English Separatist Tradition*, pp. 98f., 113–15, 127–9, 142–55.

9 Michael MacCarthy-Morrough, *The Munster Plantation. English Migration to Southern Ireland 1583–1641* (Oxford, 1986), p. 198.

10 J.S. Reid, *History of the Presbyterian Church in Ireland*, ed. W.D. Killen (3 vols., Belfast, 1867), i, 122; Samuel M'Skimin, *The History and Antiquities ... of Carrickfergus* (Belfast, 1823), 248; Daniel Neal, *The History of the Puritans* (London, 1754), i, 474; Dexter, *Congregationalism*, p. 648 n. 97; Burrage, *Early English Dissenters*, i, 201, ii, 305f; Murray Tolmie, *The Triumph of the Saints* (London, 1977), p. 37.

11 Reid, *Presbyterian Church*, i, 128f.; W. Row (ed), *The Life of Mr Robert Blair, Minister of St Andrews, containing his Autobiography, from 1593 to 1636* (s.l., 1848), pp. 83f.

12 Anthony Wood, *Athenae Oxoniensis*, ed. P. Bliss (5 vols., London 1813–15), iii, 1067;

Yet, despite this exchange of personnel, and despite the clear evidence for its external origins, it would nevertheless be wrong to see Irish dissent as simply a mirror image of its English sister. The particular, not to mention peculiar, conditions of Ireland meant that the development of the Reformation, after its early legislative plagiarism, subtly diverged from the English model. For a start there is the little matter of the failure of the Irish Protestant religion to win support. In the face of Catholic strength, Protestant unity became of prime importance. Nonconformists, far from threatening the established church, were welcomed as anti-Catholic evangelists. Sheer pragmatism also dictated tolerance. The desperate shortage of Protestant preachers in Ireland meant that the church would have been foolish to reject godly ministers who offered their services. There was no Irish Whitgift.

Somewhat surprisingly, there is no evidence that English Presbyterians tried to establish their disciplinary system in Ireland. This was probably largely the result of the timing of their arrival, after the definitive collapse of the movement in England. Thus Walter Travers, when appointed provost of Trinity College, was specifically warned by Archbishop Adam Loftus of Dublin of the dangers of innovation, and the need to respect the existing church settlement. Where such immigrants did, however, influence the development of the Irish church was in its theological stance. For when the Irish church finally got round to preparing a detailed confession of faith in 1615, it differed in a number of important respects from the Thirty Nine Articles, with the inclusion of the Lambeth Articles and the identification of the pope as Antichrist marking the Church of Ireland as more clearly Calvinist and firmly anti-Catholic.[13]

The result was that the Irish church was more inclusive than the English. Though individual bishops and visitors, particularly those recently arrived from England, periodically complained about puritan practices, few steps were taken to limit comprehension: there was no subscription in Ireland—no tests to weed out nonconformist ministers at ordination or institution. Such tolerance may well explain the lack of a continuous Separatist tradition in the early seventeenth century, and the absence of Puritan complaints and Presbyterian *classes*.[14] English Puritans blended seamlessly into the Calvinist Irish church, resulting in a remarkably homogenous institution.

A.G. Matthews (ed.), *Calamy Revised* (Oxford, 1988), p. 468; H.M.C., *Hastings MSS*, iv, 73.

13 R.B. Knox, 'The Ecclesiastical Policy of James Ussher, Archbishop of Armagh', London University, PhD thesis, 1956, pp. 69–95; R.B. Knox, *James Ussher Archbishop of Armagh* (Cardiff, 1967), pp. 16–19; Alan Ford, *The Protestant Reformation in Ireland, 1590–1641* (Frankfurt, 1987), pp. 194–201.

14 It was in fact subsequently alleged that Ainsworth, while in Ireland, had conformed to the Church of Ireland: John Paget, *An Arrow against the Separation of the Brownists* (Amsterdam, 1618), pp. 92f.

II

So far we have only examined two parts of the geographical nexus—Ireland and England—that gave rise to the Church of Ireland and to Irish dissent, or to be more precise, the absence of Irish dissent. There was, however, a third, strikingly different, model for a Reformation ecclesiastical settlement, that of Scotland. Knox and Melville's creation of a Reformed Kirk, founded upon the Bible (as interpreted by Calvin) constituted a standing challenge to the cosy compromises of the Irish ecclesiastical polity. The very name given to the early constitution of the Scottish church—the Book of Discipline, points clearly to the determination to construct from the ground up a Presbyterian style of church government which the godly in England could only envy. At the same time, however, the form and structure of the Scottish church was far from simple or fixed. There was a continuous process of adaptation, development and challenge, as cautious but determined efforts were made by James to impose, on top of this structure, an episcopal system of government. The result was a curious compromise, never without its inherent tensions, as the true locus of authority was disputed both within the church and between church and state, as bishops sought to establish themselves within the system of presbyteries.[15]

The Scottish influence on the development of the Protestant religion in Ireland in the sixteenth century was largely confined to the presence in Ireland of individual Scots who chose to make their careers there. It is true that John Knox in the 1560s had contact with Archbishop Loftus, but this, like, indeed, the presence of Scots clerics in Ireland, was much more concerned with the incestuous politics of the three kingdoms than with ecclesiological imperialism.[16] Thus both Denis Cambell, Dean of Limerick and, at the time of his death in 1603, bishop-elect of Derry, another minister, Robert Maxwell, and two Scots schoolteachers in Dublin, James Fullerton and James Hamilton acted as agents for Scottish and, in the case of Campbell, English interests.[17] Such individuals could nevertheless shape the development of institutions. Fullerton, like Hamilton a graduate of Glasgow university, was a friend of the Scottish Presbyterian leader, Andrew Melville, and played a key role in the

15 Gordon Donaldson, *The Faith of the Scots* (London, 1990); W.R. Foster, *The Church before the Covenants. The Church of Scotland 1596–1638* (Edinburgh, 1975); I.B. Cowan, *The Scottish Reformation. Church and Society in Sixteenth-Century Scotland* (London, 1982).

16 H.H.W. Robinson-Hammerstein, *Erzbischof Adam Loftus und die elizabethanische Reformationspolitik in Irland* (Marburg, 1976), pp. 77–82.

17 H.M.C. Salisbury MSS, xv, p. 64; Michael Perceval-Maxwell, *The Scottish Migration to Ulster in the Reign of James I* (London, 1990), p. 2; the suggestion that Fullerton and Hamilton were actually sent to Dublin by James VI as his agents has little foundation.

early years of Trinity College, Dublin. Indeed, both settled in Ireland permanently, and Hamilton became a major landowner in Ulster in the early seventeenth century, being made viscount Clandeboye in 1622.[18]

But the efforts of individual Scots were not backed up by any sizeable Scots Protestant presence in Ireland. For, though there was a significant number of Scots in north-east Ulster, they were predominantly from highland, Catholic clans. Thus, at the death of Elizabeth, there were 8 English and 10 Irish or Anglo-Irish Church of Ireland bishops, but none from Scotland. What transformed the position of Scots in the Church of Ireland was the immigration of the early seventeenth century, both as part of the official plantation of Ulster, and in the unofficial plantation of the two closest counties to Scotland, Down and Antrim. This produced a sizeable Scots population, of about 14,000 adults, which, crucially, mostly consisted of lowland Protestants.[19]

The sheer size of the Scottish presence, and its concentration in several key Ulster dioceses, Down and Connor, Clogher and Raphoe, utterly changed the Scots relationship to and role within the Church of Ireland. By the early seventeenth century, it is no longer a matter of tracing the careers of scattered Scots adventurers. Whole parishes were now dominated by Scots settlers, who in turn brought with them Scots clergy. These, in turn, were appointed to benefices in, and served in the Church of Ireland. Thus by 1622, out of eighteen clergy in the diocese of Down, ten were from Scotland, while in Connor thirteen out of twenty-one were Scots. In the diocese of Raphoe on the west coast of Ireland, another centre of Scots settlement, sixteen out of twenty-six clergy were Scottish.[20] Moreover, a Scots King, advised by Scottish courtiers, was much more willing to promote such ministers to positions of influence. The result was already evident by the beginning of Irish convocation in 1613, when there were three Scottish bishops, a number which doubled by the time of the next Convocation in 1634.[21] The impact was greatest where Scottish settlement was densest—in the east of Ulster, nearest to Scotland, in the combined dioceses of Down and Connor. After 1612, three successive Scots were appointed to the see, and as many as two-thirds of the clergy appointed to benefices between 1613 and 1635 were Scots.[22]

18 John Durkan and James Kirk, *The University of Glasgow 1451–1577* (Glasgow, 1977), pp. 304, 353, 381, 383.
19 Perceval-Maxwell, *Scottish Migration*, pp. 289, 250f; Raymond Gillespie, *Colonial Ulster: the Settlement of East Ulster, 1600–1641* (Cork, 1985), pp. 50–3.
20 TCD, MSS 1067; Perceval-Maxwell, *Scottish Migration*, app. F.
21 1613: Montgomery, Echlin, Knox; 1634: Spottiswood, Echlin, Leslie, Hamilton, Heygate, Adair.; T.W. Moody, F.X. Martin and F.J. Byrne (eds), *A New History of Ireland. Maps, Genealogies, Lists. A Companion to Irish History, part II* (vol. ix, Oxford, 1984), pp. 393–438.
22 S.A. Millsop, 'The State of the Church in the Diocese of Down and Connor during

What impact did this Scots presence have upon the Church of Ireland? The answer to this is complicated, and far from straightforward, since it represents the confluence of two inherently ambiguous ecclesiastical settlements. The tensions of the Scottish church were exported to Ireland with its clergy and laity, where, in turn, they encountered, and tested to the full, the flexibility of Church of Ireland. The intricacy of this relationship can be seen most simply in terms of personalities and their attitudes. At one extreme were the enthusiastic supporters of episcopacy, men such as Robert Maxwell, appointed Archdeacon of Down in 1628, or Henry Leslie, successively a prebendary in Connor in 1619, Dean of Down in 1628 and finally bishop of Down and Connor in 1635.[23] The latter, an ally of that staunch Caroline Bishop of Ross, John Maxwell , saw his role in Ireland in a similar light to Archbishop John Spottiswood in Scotland, as an obedient servant of his monarch in enforcing conformity.[24] At the other extreme were ministers for whom the changes James imposed upon the Scottish church, and the consequent pressure for their conformity, proved too much, leading them to seek refuge in the more lax climate of Ireland. Edward Brice, an Edinburgh graduate and minister at Dryburn in Stirling, settled in Ireland in 1613 as curate of Templecorran in Down and Connor, having run foul of Archbishop Spottiswood.[25] Much more significant in the history of Irish dissent was the forceful and eloquent Robert Blair, who, because of his hostility to the Perth Articles of 1618, was forced to resign from his teaching post in Glasgow University, and found employment in Ireland as Vicar of Bangor. In 1624 two ministers in Scotland, George Dunbar and Richard Dickson, who, despite their deprivations for nonconformity had continued to preach, were banished to Ireland. There is no evidence that Dickson ever came to Ireland, but Dunbar became minister at Invermore in 1624 and remained there for ten years.[26] Soon after, Blair, on a visit to Scotland, persuaded Josias Welsh, grandson of John Knox,

the Episcopate of Robert Echlin 1613–35', Queens' University Belfast, M.A. thesis, 1979, 275f.

23 John Leslie, *A treatise of the authority of the church* (Dublin, 1637), sig. **4r.

24 D.N.B.; SP 63/252/121 fols 235r–236r (*CSPI*, 1625–32, p. 629); Row (ed.), *Life of Blair*, p. 90.

25 He was one of only two ministers to oppose Spottiswood's nomination as permanent moderator of the synod of Clydesdale, and subsequently was charged with adultery. He is rather inaccurately termed the 'first presbyterian minister in Ireland': Patrick Adair, *A True Narrative of the Rise and Progress of the Presbyterian Church in Ireland 1623–70*, ed. W.D. Killen (Belfast, 1866), p. 1; Representative Church Body Library, Dublin: J.B.Leslie, 'Connor Clergy', p. 55; [D. Laing] (ed.), *Original Letters relating to the Ecclesiastical Affairs of Scotland* (Edinburgh, 1851), i, 105; Perceval-Maxwell, *Scottish Migration*, p. 269.

26 [Laing] (ed), *Original Letters*, ii, 762, 766f.; Row (ed), *Life of Blair*, pp. 75f.; Adair, *A True Narrative*, p. 21; G.I.R. McMahon, 'The Scottish courts of High Commission 1610–38' in *Records of the Scottish Church History Society*, xv (1966), pp. 200f.

and firm opponent of prelacy, to join him in Ireland. Another principled emigrant was John Livingstone, educated at Glasgow University under, as he put it in his autobiography, 'the oversight of precious Mr Robert Blair'. Having been 'from my infancy bred with averseness from episcopacy and ceremonies', Livingstone found the Articles of Perth unacceptable.[27] Though called to several parishes, his efforts to secure an appointment were, he felt, blocked by the bishops. After a spell as an itinerant preacher in Scotland, he came to Ireland in 1630 to serve in the parish of Killinchy in the diocese of Down and Connor.[28]

What these ministers were exploiting, of course, was the liberality of the Irish church settlement which allowed conformists and nonconformists to co-exist provided probing questions about issues such as discipline and ceremonies were studiously avoided. The compromises by which these ministers operated in Ireland were vividly described in their autobiographies, and depended upon a conscious exercise in ambiguity. Blair, on his arrival in Ireland, was assured by his patron that, despite his reluctance to submit to 'episcopal government ... [or] any part of the English liturgy', there would be no difficulty in securing his admission to the ministry.[29] Indeed, according to Blair's own account he specifically warned the bishop of Down and Connor, Robert Echlin, of his reservations. 'Notwithstanding he was most willing I should be planted there'.[30] With regard to the crucial and sensitive issue of ordination, Echlin, as Blair recounted it, suggested a compromise:

> 'Whatever you account of episcopacy, yet I know you account a presbyter to have divine warrant; will you not receive ordination from Mr Cunningham and the adjacent brethren, and let me come in amongst them in no other relation than a presbyter?' This I could not refuse, and so that matter was performed.[31]

According to Livingstone's account he was advised by his patron not to seek ordination from Bishop Robert Echlin of Down and Connor, who, it was thought, would by this stage require some commitment to conformity of him, but instead to obtain orders from Andrew Knox, the aged Scottish bishop of Raphoe. Knox, according to Livingstone's account, 'gave me the book of ordination, and desired that anything that I scrupled at I should draw a line

27 'The Life of Mr John Livingstone, Minister of the Gospel', in W.K. Tweedie (ed.), *Select Biographies* (Edinburgh, 1847), pp. 129–33; McMahon, 'High Commission', p. 200.
28 Tweedie (ed), *Select Biographies*, pp. 134ff.
29 Row (ed), *Life of Blair*, pp. 51, 54.
30 Ibid., p. 58.
31 Ibid., p. 59.

over it in the margin ... but I found that it had been so marked by some others before that I needed not mark anything'.[32] He then required him to preach a sermon and afterwards joined with three or four other Scottish clergy in the laying on of hands.

The question of ordination is obviously a key one for the Scottish clergy who came over to Ireland. Two ministers, Edward Brice and George Dunbar, and, indeed, Bishop Echlin himself, are known to have been ordained by presbytery in Scotland, and the Irish church seems to have followed the example of the Scottish in accepting their orders as valid.[33] In the case of the vast majority of other ministers, because of their failure to secure a benefice in Scotland and possibly as a result of their concern that their ordination should be linked to their call to ministry, they were not ordained until after their arrival in Ireland.[34] Indeed, of fourteen nonconformists in 1634 for whom details of ordination are available, two (Brice and Dunbar) were ordained in Scotland, one in England, while the remaining eleven were ordained by Ulster bishops, nine of them by Echlin.[35]

The vital point to note here, of course, is the possible ambiguity inherent in Blair's ordination. Viewed at from the perspective of the bishop, his ordination was, arguably, thoroughly orthodox. It was perfectly normal in the Church of Ireland ordinal for ministers present to join with the bishop in the laying on of hands.[36] Thus the records of the Church of Ireland simply record that Blair was ordained deacon and priest on 10 July 1623 by Echlin.[37] The one piece of damning evidence in Blair's account—that the bishop knew when ordaining him that he was hostile to both episcopacy and the Book of Common Prayer—was flatly contradicted by Echlin in an account he gave of Blair's ordination in 1632.[38] It is therefore possible to claim that, while the ministers believed, with some justification, that they had been presbyterially ordained, bishop Echlin had equal grounds for portraying his ordination of Blair as conforming to the rites of the established church.

An even more uneasy compromise was arrived it in relation to ecclesiastical discipline. The general ineffectiveness and corruption of the ecclesiastical

32 Tweedie (ed), *Select Biographies*, p. 141.
33 TCD, MS 1067, p. 95; a further two ministers were probably ordained in Scotland: Andrew Stewart and James Glendinning: J.T. Barkley, *A Short History of the Presbyterian Church in Ireland* (Belfast, 1959), p. 4; J.M. Barkley, 'Some Scottish Bishops and Ministers in the Irish Church, 1605–35', in Duncan Shaw (ed), *Reformation and Revolution. Essays presented to ... Hugh Watt* (Edinburgh, 1967), p. 143.
34 The best discussion of the issue of ordination is in Knox, *James Ussher*, pp. 177–86.
35 Shefflied City Library, Wentworth Woodhouse Muniments [hereafter W.W.M.], vol. 20/179; TCD, MS 1067, pp. 88–105.
36 Knox, *James Ussher*, p. 180.
37 TCD, MS 1034, pp. 100f.
38 SP 63/253/2116 (*CSPI*, 1625–32, pp. 661f.).

courts was a serious handicap for the Irish Reformation.[39] The episcopal cession of authority to the canon lawyers, even, as in Down and Connor, to the widow of a local landowner, made it extremely difficult to fashion the courts into an effective instrument for ecclesiastical discipline.[40] What the Scottish clergy offered was an alternative model, not the product of any overarching diocesan or even synodal authority, but firmly founded upon the parish, based not on canon law and a complex system of fees and fines, but upon the enforcement of a biblically based moral code by Calvinist pastors and locally appointed elders.[41] Livingstone gave a detailed account of the system and its operation in his parish of Killinchy:

> Not only had we the public worship free of any inventions of men, but we had also a tolerable discipline; for after I had been some while amongst them, by the advice of all the heads of families, some ablest for that charge were chosen elders to oversee the manners of the rest, and some deacons to gather and distribute the collection. we met every week, and such as fell in notorious public scandals were desired to come before us. Such as came we dealt with both in public and private, and prevailed with to confess their scandals before the congregation, at the Saturday sermon before the communion, which was twice in the year, and then were admitted to the communion. Such as after dealing either would not come before us, or coming would not be convinced to confess their fault before the congregation, their names, and scandals, and impenitency, was read out before the congregation, and they debarred from the communion, which proved such a terror, that we found very few of that sort.[42]

Given the fact that the Scottish ministers were attempting to create this alternative system like a Trojan horse within the framework of the Church of Ireland, a clash was almost inevitable. The catalyst in Blair's parish was a rich young heir who, resentful at being castigated by the ministers and elders for public scandal, appealed to the bishop 'whereby the order of that discipline was broken'.[43]

39 Alan Ford, 'The Reformation in Kilmore to 1641', in Raymond Gillespie (ed), *Cavan: an Irish County History* (Dublin, 1995).
40 TCD, MS 550, p. 244.
41 Gillespie, *Colonial Ulster*, p. 160.
42 Tweedie (ed), *Select Biographies*, p. 142.
43 Adair, *True Narrative*, p. 12; Row (ed), *Life of Blair*, pp. 68f.

III

It will already be apparent that the crucial intermediaries, who enabled the Scots to be incorporated within the framework of the established church, were the local landlords and the Scottish bishops. Just as in England, where the gentry had been crucial in sustaining Puritan ideals at a parish level, so too in Down and Connor, it was the Scots and English settlers that played a similar supporting role. Four distinct elements combined to enhance the ecclesiastical influence of the leading settlers. First, the distance of north-east Ulster from Dublin and London meant that, especially in the first two decades of the plantation, official interference, even interest, in the functioning of the church in Down and Connor was limited. Second, the power of patronage was concentrated in lay hands. In some Ulster dioceses, as, for example, in Kilmore, most of the benefices were collative—in the presentation of the bishop.[44] But in Down and Connor 65 out of the 75 livings listed in the 1634 visitation were in lay hands.[45] Moreover, as the settlers built up and consolidated their land holdings, by fair means and foul, they included in their predations church livings, swallowing up the income from benefices, replacing independently endowed vicars and rectors with dependent curates.[46] Finally, having acquired this influence over the church, a significant section of the landholders were not averse to using it to secure employment for nonconformist ministers. Here we again encounter James Hamilton, now viscount Clandeboye. It was he who actively sought out Blair and Livingstone in Scotland, invited them to serve in Ireland, secured the ordination of Blair by Echlin and pointed Livingstone in the direction of Knox.[47] Indeed, Clandeboye is known to have been the patron of at least seven nonconformist Scots clergy in Down and Connor, including his own nephew, James.[48] Other nonconformist clergy found similar support from the planters. James Montgomery presented his namesake (a relative by marriage of his wife) to Grey Abbey in 1633.[49] William Edmonston another Scots planter, presented Edward Brice to Kilroot in 1613. And, as Scots settlers attracted Scots Presbyterian clergy, so

---

44 Ford, 'The Reformation in Kilmore'.
45 Millsop, 'Diocese of Down and Connor', p. 245.
46 TCD, MS 550, pp. 244–61; S.P. 63/254/185 (*CSPI*, 1633–47, 87f.); E.P. Shirley (ed), *Papers Relating to the Church of Ireland (1631–9)* (London and Dublin, [1874]), p. 41; W.W.M., vol. 20/179.
47 Row (ed), *Life of Blair*, p. 51; Tweedie (ed), *Select Biographies*, p. 141.
48 W.W.M., vol. 20/179; T.K.Lowry (ed), *The Hamilton Manuscripts* (Belfast, 1867), pp. 33f, 74f.; Row (ed), *Life of Blair*, p. 64; Millsop, 'Diocese of Down and Connor', pp. 317–19, 321–3, 326; Blair (Bangor), Boyle (Killyleagh), Cunningham (Holywood), Hamilton (Ballywalter), Alexander Forbes (Blaris), Livingston (Killinchy), Porteous (Ballyhalbert).
49 Millsop, 'Diocese of Down and Connor', pp. 283f.

English settlers were associated with English Puritans: Sir Arthur Chichester, the former Lord Deputy, presented John Ridge to Antrim, while Robert Langford presented Henry Calvert to Muckamore.[50] Josias Welsh was first employed in Ireland as a household chaplain to the Welsh settler, Humphrey Norton.[51] Nor were the ministers limited to local patrons. John Bole or Boyle, a blind Scots nonconformist cleric whom Clandeboye presented to four rectories in Down, also looked to the earl of Cork, one of the Lords Justices, for support.[52]

One respected authority has suggested that there was Puritan network of prominent English settlers, including Chichester, the Clotworthys and Nortons, that was based upon Carrickfergus and south Antrim.[53] There is no doubt that Carrickfergus had always been a Protestant bastion in Ulster, but it would be wrong make too firm a connection between the views of the clergy and those of their patrons. The Clotworthys were indeed firmly Puritan, even Presbyterian, in their sympathies, but they possessed hardly any patronage in the diocese. Though Chichester and Clandeboye were clearly sympathetic to nonconformist clergy—quite possibly a product of their backgrounds—neither can be described themselves as nonconformist.[54] Bramhall in 1634 thought that patrons of nonconformist ministers were concerned solely with the plantation of their lands, 'and that work being done, are indifferent ... what becomes of them'.[55] Blair, in fact, acknowledges that his patron did not share his detestation of kneeling at communion, and Clandeboye in the later 1630s proved quite willing to co-operate with the authorities in weeding out nonconformity in Down and Connor.[56] At the same time, however, Clandeboye proved willing to shelter nonconformist ministers from the authorities in his own home.[57] This Janus-like quality was passed on to his son, who succeeded in 1643, and was described by the family historian: 'His education and conversation inclined him to be episcopal; but he was therein very moderate, and paid a great respect to all good persons and was in his practice Presbyterian'.[58]

50 TCD MS 1067, p. 96
51 Andrew Stewart, *The History of the Church in Ireland since the Scots were Naturalized*, ed. W.D. Killen (Belfast, 1866), p. 318.
52 TCD, MS 1067, p. 88; NLI MS 13,237/26.
53 A.F.S. Pearson, Puritan and Presbyterian Settlements in Ireland 1560–1660 (Typescript in The Presbyterian Historical Society of Ireland, Belfast), pp. 139, 174.
54 John McCavitt, 'The Lord Deputyship of Sir Arthur Chichester in Ireland, 1605–16', Queen's University Belfast, PhD thesis, 1988, p. 1; Lowry (ed), *Hamilton Manuscripts*, pp. 31f.
55 S.P. 63/254/185 (*CSPI, 1633–47,* 87f.); E.P. Shirley (ed), *Papers relating to the Church of Ireland (1631–9)* (London and Dublin, 1874]), p. 41.
56 Row (ed), *Life of Blair*, p. 61; Michael Perceval-Maxwell, 'Strafford, the Ulster Scots and the Covenanters' in *I.H.S.*, xviii, no 72 (Sept. 1973), p. 547.
57 Lowry (ed), *Hamilton Manuscripts*, p. 35.
58 Ibid., p. 71.

At the centre of this network of ambivalence was, of course, the bishop, Robert Echlin. Early in his episcopate, safe from the gaze of the authorities in Dublin and London, he seems to have been prepared to go to considerable lengths to accommodate Scots ministers. When, in 1632, he had to explain to the Dublin authorities why he had allowed Blair, Livingstone, Dunbar and Welsh to minister in his diocese, he lamely and revealingly claimed that he had restricted them to curacies, had only permitted them to continue to preach because he had hope of their conformity and that they were, besides, attracting considerable audiences.[59] Certainly the accounts of Echlin's personality by nonconformist clergy do not suggest that he was seen as strict by choice, but rather that he would take the easiest course open to him. In the eyes of John Ridge, the English Puritan minister at Antrim, Echlin was 'not malicious, yet willing to strike all rather than to adventure himself to a blow'.[60] This judgement was shared by one of his episcopalian colleagues: though far from the nonconformists doctrinally, 'yet he is of so timorous a disposition that he is loath to take upon him the envy of the people'.[61]

Presiding over this curious compromise was James Ussher, the Irish-born archbishop of Armagh. Ussher's chief modern biographer has sought to dissociate the primate from any hint of collusion with the Presbyterian ordinations, determinedly showing that Ussher was a firm Anglican.[62] Nonconformists, however, have repeatedly sought to enlist Ussher as a sympathetic supporter.[63] Thus Blair gives a pointed account of his amicable discussions with the primate in his palace at Drogheda.[64] Baxter nostalgically placed Ussher amongst the 'Old Episcopal Divines', who were flexible on the subject of ordination by presbyters rather than bishops, in marked contrast to the 'new episcopal divines', such as Bramhall and Laud who 'unchurch those churches that are not prelatical'.[65] Ussher's willingness in the early 1640s, when the London Parliament was threatening the very basis of the English ecclesiastical settlement, to consider, in *The reduction of episcopacy*, a disciplinary system which merged bishops and ministers in a 'kind of presbyterial government' appears to lend support to Blair's and Baxter's judgements.[66] In fact, however, Ussher

59 SP 63/253/2116 (*CSPI*, 1625–32, pp. 661f.).
60 NLI, MS 8014/i.
61 SP 63/252/121 fols 235v (*CSPI*, 1625–32, p. 629).
62 Knox, James Ussher, pp. 16–23, 167–89.
63 T.C. Barnard, *Cromwellian Ireland. English Government and Reform in Ireland 1649–1660* (Oxford, 1975), pp. 91f.
64 Reid, *Presbyterian Church*, i, 136f.; Row (ed.), *Life of Blair*, pp. 80f.
65 Richard Baxter, *Five Disputations of Church Government and Worship* (London, 1659), quoted in J.W. Packer, *The Transformation of Anglicanism 1643–1660 with special reference to Henry Hammond* (Manchester, 1969), pp. 197f.
66 James Ussher, *The Whole Works*, C.R. Elrington and J.H. Todd (eds) (17 vols., Dublin, London, 1847–64), xii, 533.

was neither an Anglican—use of that term in relation to the English, let alone the Irish, church in the early seventeenth century is utterly anachronistic— nor was he a Presbyterian fellow traveller. He was a stout defender of the Church of Ireland's distinctive ecclesiastical settlement, including its reluctance to impose subscription on ministers, but was at the same time utterly loyal to its supreme governor and deeply respectful of the power of the king and his ministers—hence his reluctance to publish his *Reduction of episcopacy* when it became evident that the king was unsympathetic.[67]

What forced Ussher and Echlin to confront the issue of nonconformity in the 1630s was the determination of Henry Leslie to bring the aberrations in the diocese to the attention of the authorities not just in Dublin but in London, and the increasing desire of those authorities to abandon the ecclesiastical *modus vivendi* of the early seventeenth century in favour of much closer conformity with the English religious settlement. Leslie had shrewdly attached himself to the rising star of that great stickler for conformity and 'new episcopal divine', William Laud, bishop of London.[68] In 1631 he formally complained about the activities of Blair and Livingstone to the Lords Justices in Dublin telling them how he had expostulated with Echlin and Clandeboye 'for winking at this disorder, protesting that I would complain to the state and procure a certificate of their irregularities to be transmitted unto England'. Leslie ensured that action was taken against the ministers through civil courts with the help of Sir Richard Bolton, Chief Baron of the Exchequer, and a firm opponent of nonconformity.[69] This finally forced Echlin's hand, and he suspended Blair, Livingstone, Welsh and George Dunbar.

The ministers, rather shocked at the sudden move after enjoying their 'full liberty' for so long, responded in two ways: first they looked at the possibility of compromise—faced with the traditional Puritan dilemma of abandoning their principles or their flock, they hoped 'that some small thing (small in respect of the whole course of conformity) would, at least for a while, give content'.[70] Second, they sought to mobilise as much support as they could to press the authorities to let the matter drop. Appeal to Archbishop Ussher secured a brief remission.[71] But in May 1632 the ministers were sentenced to be deprived.[72] At this point the focus shifted to the English court. The

---

67 Ford, 'A Puritan Church', p. 67; W.M. Abbott, 'James Ussher and "Ussherian" episcopacy, 1640–1656: the primate and his *Reduction* manuscript' in *Albion*, xxii (1990), pp. 237–59.
68 SP 63/249/1485 (*CSPI*, 1625–32, p. 481); SP 63/252/121 fols 235r–236r (C.S.P.I., 1625–32, p. 629).
69 SP 63/252/121 fols 235r–236r (CSPI, 1625–32, p. 629); Row (ed), *Life of Blair*, p. 90; Tweedie (ed), *Select Biographies*, p. 145; NLI, MS 8014/i.
70 NLI, MS 8014/i.
71 For a discussion of Ussher's attitude, see Ford 'A Puritan Church?', pp. 65f.
72 Row (ed), *Life of Blair*, p. 91; Tweedie (ed), *Select Biographies*, p. 145.

ministers could call on their considerable and powerful Scottish connections, and Blair himself went to court and secured a letter from the King which, while not favourable, was not hostile either, referring the dispute to the Irish Lords Justices for adjudication.[73]

The evil day was, by various shifts, postponed until 1634, but in that year the very nature of conformity, and the disciplinary framework of the Church of Ireland was fundamentally changed, as the new Lord Deputy, Thomas Wentworth, acting on the advice of his ally William Laud, the Archbishop of Canterbury, imposed his will on the church. Sweeping aside the reservations of Ussher and other Irish churchmen, Wentworth ensured that Convocation in 1634 in effect replaced the Irish Articles by the English, and for the first time imposed a set of Canons, based upon those of 1604 in England, upon the Irish church. The result was that clergy had for the first time to subscribe to the Thirty-Nine Articles and the Book of Common Prayer. Consequently the bishops of the Church of Ireland, urged on by Wentworth and Laud, finally were equipped with the essential weapons with which they could fight nonconformity. These weapons were indeed used in Down and Connor. Wentworth commanded the bishop to order the recalcitrant ministers to conform by 1 November, trying in the meantime to convince them by personal conference.[74] A regal visitation of the diocese in 1634, led by Bramhall, identified 20 nonconformist ministers, and five preaching schoolmasters. Some of these, Bramhall hoped, might submit, but others he categorised as 'desperate nonconformists'.[75] Over the next seven years the persistent nonconformists were deprived and even driven out from Ireland, most of them returning to Scotland.[76] Their chief persecutor was Henry Leslie, who, when Echlin died in 1635, was the obvious royal choice to succeed him.[77]

The most recent and reliable analysis of Wentworth's Ulster policy has claimed that 'by the middle of 1637, Wentworth and Leslie had been largely successful in their campaign against the ministers in Down and Connor, and were in a position to bring pressure to bear on nonconforming laymen'.[78] In institutional terms, this may be true. But looking beyond the institutional history of who was dismissed when, to the broader history of popular Protestant piety, the impact of the Scottish ministers extends well beyond 1637. They contributed something of major importance not just to the history of

---

73 Perceval-Maxwell, 'Strafford, the Ulster Scots and the Covenanters', p. 525; H.M.C., *Cowper MSS*, i, 469.
74 W.W.M. vol. 8, p. 102.
75 W.W.M. vol. 20/179.
76 Reid, *Presbyterian Church*, i, ch. 4.
77 For details of dates of deprivation see Millsop, 'Diocese of Down and Connor', pp. 316ff.
78 Perceval-Maxwell, 'Strafford, the Ulster Scots and the Covenanters', p. 528.

dissent in Ireland, but also to the broader tradition of Protestant religiosity, and, more specifically to the way in which Reformed theology was related in Ireland to religious feeling and practice.

Recent work on the impact of the Reformation in England has resulted in a radical reappraisal of the power and coherence of pre-Reformation piety. This has been a valuable corrective to the Foxean tradition of English religious history which, in the light of this research, now appears to have been overly dismissive of the popular appeal of Catholicism.[79] However, this reappraisal has been achieved at the expense of a certain imbalance. As the richness of Catholic piety has emerged, with its fusion of sight and sound, this world and the next, the living and the dead in a warm, all-enveloping communal religion, Protestant piety has, tended to be defined antithetically, as a word based, Bible-centred, iconoclastic individualistic piety associated with a cold self-analytical intellectualism. Taken to extremes, such an approach makes it difficult to explain the mass acceptance of the Protestant religion as anything other than an imposition by the state upon an unwilling populace.

The wider significance of the events in Down and Connor in the early seventeenth century is that they offer a rare—indeed I would argue the first—insight into the nature and development of popular Protestant piety in Ireland. One point which repeatedly emerges from the accounts of both conformists and their opponents in Down and Connor is that the Scots clergy won considerable local support and esteem. Blair records his ceaseless round of preaching, catechism, instruction and prayer and the positive response from the 1,200 adults in his parish.[80] When Livingstone arrived in 1630 he was initially worried about his lack of pastoral impact.[81] But he soon encountered the popular enthusiasm for the gospel, concluding that 'I do not think there were more lively and experienced Christians any where than were these at that time in Ireland, and that in good numbers ...'[82] Ridge, as an Englishman, viewed the matter from the perspective of a sympathetic outsider, yet, writing to a fellow Puritan in Oxfordshire, he came to a similarly positive conclusion:

> Round about there are divers Scottish ministers that Scotland would not bear because of their nonconformity ... These are such men for strict walking and abundant pains with their people Sabbath day, week days, in church and from house to house that I have never ... known of

79 J.J. Scarisbrick, *The Reformation and the English People* (Oxford, 1984); Eamon Duffy, *The Stripping of the Altars. Traditional Religion in England c.1400–c.1580* (New Haven, 1992); Christopher Haigh, *English Reformations. Religion, Politics, and Society under the Tudors* (Oxford, 1993).
80 Row (ed), *Life of Blair*, pp. 59, 63f.
81 Tweedie (ed), *Select Biographies*, pp. 141f.
82 Ibid., p. 144.

> any more heavenly in their conversation or more laborious in their ministry, and unto this they have a very sweet encouragement, for the Lord hath exceedingly blessed their labours for they have brought a great number of people for 20 miles about them to as great a measure of knowledge and zeal in every good duty, as, I think, is to be found again in any part of Christendom ... Their congregations are some 7 or 800, some 1000, some 1,500, some more some less ...

Moreover, the public efforts of the clergy had their effect within the community. Ridge specifically commented how 'the people have a notable commerce one with another, people with people, family with family, one private Christian with others, and being thus constant in their fervency and spiritual trading, the work comes on mightily among them'.[83]

These sources are, of course, self-serving, part of a familiar Puritan genre, painting an heroic picture of the labours of the godly saints. But even the hostile Leslie also noted the boundless popular enthusiasm for the Scots ministers.[84] Indeed, even after their expulsion, he conceded that he was facing an uphill struggle in reclaiming his flock. He was, he confessed in 1636, amazed at their continued following amongst the people—'for every one of these presbyterial dictators is more esteemed than the whole church of God', and rather plaintively noted that despite his efforts to root out nonconformist zeal 'as yet I have not found either my pains or my prayers to be so effectual.[85] Even in 1638 he was still complaining about 'both ... the clergy and the laity, for their general non-conformity, and disobedience unto the orders of this church'.[86]

Indeed it is quite clear that the ministry of the Scots clergy gained more than support and esteem, it aroused mass enthusiasm. Their efforts created in 1626 the first recorded example of what was to become a notable feature of Scottish, Scots-Irish and, in due course, American religious culture—the popular revival, that organised movement of religious enthusiasm that culminated in the Great Awakening of the eighteenth century.[87] Blair and Livingstone give a meticulous account of the origins of the revival. Founded upon the two main marks of Calvin's church: the preaching of the gospel and the administration of the sacraments, it began in the valley of the Six Mile Water in

---

83 NLI, MS 8014/i.

84 SP 63/252/121 fol 235r (*CSPI, 1625–32*, p. 629).

85 Leslie, *Authority of the Church*, sig. *3v, *2v.

86 Henry Leslie, *A Speech Delivered at the Visitation of Downe and Conner: held in Lisnegarvy the 26th of September, 1638: wherein, for the Convincing of the Nonconformists, there is a Full Confutation of the Covenant lately Sworne and Subscribed by many in Scotland* (London, 1639), p. 3.

87 M.J. Westerkamp, *The Triumph of the Laity. Scots-Irish Piety and the Great Awakening, 1625–1760* (Oxford, 1988).

southern Antrim, the initial impetus coming from James Glendinning, a Scots minister delicately poised on the boundary between enthusiasm and madness (he was convinced that those who turned in their sleep could not be faithful Christians, and eventually left Ireland to visit the seven churches of Asia).[88] Glendinning's approach was that of a hell-fire preacher—'having a great voice and vehement delivery, he roused up the people, and wakened them with terrors'.[89] His exclusive concentration upon the misery and sinfulness of the people, and his apparent inability to preach the gospel of salvation, aroused concern in his fellow ministers, who attempted to assuage the fears that Glendinning had aroused. John Ridge, the English minister at Antrim proposed that the ministers in the Six Mile Water valley combine to provide a monthly lecture at the main town, Antrim. The result was four sermons on a set day each month in summer, three in winter, preached by Ridge, Robert Cunningham, James Hamilton and Blair. Supported by the local landlord, Sir Hugh Clotworthy, the monthly meetings were, Ridge claimed, 'constantly kept and greatly frequented'—with 1000 or 1500 people flocking there even from beyond Down and Connor.[90] In the early 1630s, 'the perpetual fear that the bishop would put away their ministers' merely heightened the people's 'great hunger' for such preaching.[91]

The essential appendage to the gospel was, of course the sacrament of the Lord's Supper. In Down and Connor the popular impact of joint preaching was strengthened by the remarkable development of a form of co-operative communion. The ministers generally celebrated the Lord's Supper but four times a year in their parish, a marked declension from Calvin's original vain hope of weekly communion in Geneva. But the concentration of Scottish settlers and ministers in southern Antrim and north Down enabled them to time each parish communion so that they could be jointly celebrated by all the surrounding parishes, thus increasing both frequency and attendance.[92] Such were the numbers attending that two sittings of communion had to be arranged in the church. Ridge spoke of '17 or 18 tables a day, each table taking about an hundred people'. Moreover, since people travelled such distances, they stayed overnight, thus offering the zealous clergy the opportunity of both preparing them for communion and further instructing them afterwards. People arrived on a Saturday to hear the evening sermon, spend much of the night in conference and prayer with the clergy attending, then heard another sermon together with communion on the Sunday, followed by a further ser-

88 Row (ed), *Life of Blair*, pp. 72, 74.
89 Ibid., p. 70.
90 Ibid., pp. 71, 84; Adair, *True Relation*, pp. 16f.; NLI, MS 8014/i.
91 Tweedie (ed), *Select Biographies*, p. 144; HMC, 10th report, app. I, *Eglinton MSS*, p. 46.
92 Row (ed), *Life of Blair*, p. 64.

mon on Sunday evening, with time to take in a 'special exhortation' on the Monday before their departure. Livingstone, the ever-optimistic preacher, claims that they left untroubled by tiredness despite their having scarcely slept.[93]

This intense activity, from 1625 to 1632, the first documented evangelical revival in Ireland, has many fascinating features. Theologically it represents a fusion of two often contradictory elements of the Reformation: word and sacrament. Though Luther and Calvin laboured to preserve the balance between them, they, or to be more precise, their followers, did not always succeed. The tendency in some reaches of the Reformed tradition to see the Lord's Supper as an occasional addendum to the centrepiece of the sermon, as a mere reminder of Christ's death, led to the sacrament taking second place. The approach of revival ministers marked a return to Calvin's original stress upon the centrality of the Lord's Supper, indeed to Calvin's vision of the sacrament as an expression of ecclesial community.[94]

Ecclesiologically the revival was a product of complex fusion of Scottish, English and Irish influences, and represents, in fascinating fashion, the collision of the three different church polities. The way in which the Scottish church exported its inherent tensions to Ireland has already been mentioned, and it impossible not to see the revival in terms of Scottish church politics. Some Ulster ministers can be identified with the 'privy kirk' tradition, a radical dissenting group within the Scottish Presbyterian church, and their efforts in Ireland were paralleled by another revival taking place in Scotland at the same time.[95] Support for the Ulster revival came overwhelmingly from Scots settlers and their Scots landlords. After Wentworth and Leslie suppressed it, the ministers, and even some of their congregations, moved back to Scotland, where they played prominent roles in the covenanting revolution.[96] At the same time, however, one must not forget the role of the English clergy and their parishioners. It was, after all, Ridge who had proposed the establishment of that typical English godly solution to a lack of preaching—the monthly lecture 'by combination'.[97] And as Ridge noted, there were tensions between the Scots and English ministers over the manner of receiving the Lord's Supper.[98] Indeed so separate were the English clergy that Josias Welsh

---

93 Ibid., pp. 84–6; Tweedie (ed), *Select Biographies*, p. 144; N.L.I. MS 8014/i.
94 B.A. Gerrish, *Grace and Gratitude. The Eucharistic Theology of John Calvin* (Edinburgh, 1993), p. 151.
95 Peter Brooke, *Ulster Presbyterianism. The historical perspective 1610–1970* (Dublin, 1987), p. 17.
96 Row (ed), *Life of Blair*, pp. 148ff.; Tweedie, *Select Biographies*, pp. 160ff.
97 On combination lectures, see Patrick Collinson, *Godly People. Essays on English Protestantism and Puritanism* (London, 1983), pp. 468f.
98 NLI, MS 8014/i.

reported in triumph in 1632 when Ridge's congregation agreed to take communion sitting rather than kneeling.[99] Finally, one has to note again the
capacity of the Irish church to absorb in the early seventeenth century the
Scottish clergy, to provide a flexible enough framework for such an experiment to be conducted. Whether or not this ecclesiological structure offered a
genuine alternative to those in Scotland and England is open to debate. On
the one hand, as early as 1623, the Archbishop of Armagh, Christopher
Hampton, had complained about the Scots in Down 'entertaining the Scottish discipline and liturgy so strongly, that they offer wrong to the church
government here established'.[100] On the other hand, his successor, James Ussher,
showed little inclination to act against nonconformity.[101]

The revival also illustrated graphically the fundamental clash between
enthusiasm and institutional structures. It broke free from the institutional
restraints of the parish system and the liturgical, disciplinary and ceremonial
requirements of the established church. The loosely structured communal
church that transcended traditional boundaries was seen by the ministers
themselves as a remarkable evangelical achievement, harnessing enthusiasm to
a scripturally based vision of the unity of word and sacrament. By their own
account, the clergy struggled repeatedly to ensure that popular enthusiasm
did not slip into heresy or delusion, seeking to distinguish true from false
faith, the work of the Lord from the counterfeiting of the devil.[102] For de-
fenders of the structures of the Church of Ireland, however, the enthusiasm
was simply out of control. It crossed the borders into fanaticism and mass
hysteria. As Leslie reported in 1632, the popular frenzies had been excited by:

> a new piece of divinity that no man can be converted unless he feels
> the pains of his new birth such as St Paul felt. So that every sermon,
> 40 or so people, for most part women, fall down in the church in a
> trance ... grievously afflicted with convulsions, trembling ... After they
> awake they confess that they have see devils ...[103]

Leslie, while bearing witness to the strength of the revival's hold on the
people, repeatedly stressed its dangerous and unstable nature, as shown by
the excessive support that the Scots ministers received from women 'in whom
there is least ability of judgement'. It was, he noted, 'by this means the
serpent overcame mankind'.[104] Hence his horrified cry, not untypical of estab-

99 HMC, *Eglinton MSS*, 10th Report, app. 1, p. 46.
100 Bodleian Library, MS Carte 30, fol. 110r.
101 See above, pp. 21f.
102 Row (ed), *Life of Blair*, pp. 74, 89.
103 SP 63/252/121 fol 235v (*CSPI*, 1625–32, p. 629).
104 Leslie, *Authority of the Church*, sig. *2r.

lishments when faced with enthusiasm: 'If these things go on, God knows what shall become of our church'.[105]

I V

The pre-history of dissent in Ireland is not, therefore, simple. There lurked within the Church of Ireland in the early seventeenth century multiple possibilities, the product of the interplay between the three kingdoms and their different but related religious settlements, and of the flexible way that the Irish church assimilated the English and Scots influences. The intervention of Wentworth, Laud and Bramhall decisively ended any distinctively Irish attempt to develop these possibilities. When Bramhall set out to reconstruct the Church of Ireland after the restoration he was determined to ensure that there should be no repetition of the earlier flexibility and ambiguity. Presbyterian ministers as a result now had to be re-ordained if they wished to serve in the Church of Ireland.[106] The boundaries of conformity had been firmly and much more narrowly defined.

But the events of Down and Connor, and the quieter work of godly ministers elsewhere in Ireland, are of wider significance than just an abortive ecclesiological experiment. They provide us with the first clear evidence of Protestant religiosity in Ireland: the first time that we can look beyond the bounds official religion and examine the practical experience of Protestantism amongst the laity. We have in Down and Connor in the 1620s and 1630s the first example not merely of organised dissent in Ireland, but of popular Protestant religious enthusiasm. Given the rather austere picture of Puritan and Protestant piety that has recently been painted, it is important to note that this manifestation was far from individualistic and had, apparently, made the transition from Calvinist theology into a popular religion, which, like Catholicism, appealed to a significant, though racially distinct, section of the population. Indeed, it is ironic that the revival's main feature—the three day eucharistic festival—can be seen as a Protestant refashioning of key elements in traditional Catholic public piety—feasts, processions, and excessive eucharistic religiosity—which were normally condemned by Reformers.[107] As one perceptive commentator has put it: 'popular festivity centering on the sacrament was rehabilitated and maintained in reformed guise'.[108]

Whether this evidence of a vital popular piety was inevitably to be associ-

---

105 SP 63/252/121 fol 235v (*CSPI*, 1625–32, p. 629).
106 Brooke, *Ulster Presbyterianism*, pp. 47f.
107 L.E. Schmidt, *Holy Fairs: Scottish Communions and American Revivals in the early Modern Period* (Princeton, 1989), p. 200.
108 Ibid., p. 213.

ated with dissent—whether, in short, such enthusiasm could only operate outside the bounds of the established church—is a difficult question to answer. One must be cautious about coming to judgements about the piety of moderate prayer-book Anglicanism within the Church of Ireland: by its very orthodoxy and moderation it removed itself from surviving records. Here too one needs to differentiate between the assumptions and approaches of the various national groups that we have identified within the Church of Ireland. As far as the English Puritans in Ireland were concerned, it would, I suspect, be wrong to identify them as a lunatic fringe. They did not see themselves as Separatists but as essential members of the national church: indeed, in their own eyes, and in the eyes of some historians, they constituted little less than the evangelical wing of the Reformation. Ridge's image of the Puritan's relationship to the rest of the Church of Ireland is conveyed in the story he tells approvingly about a conversation in which a leading Catholic told an Ulster Protestant that: 'were I to change my religion and become a protestant, I should be of you puritans, for the rest among you are of no religion'.[109]

The position of the Scottish ministers is more difficult to define. Viewed proleptically, with the knowledge both of what they went on to do in Scotland, and of how Bramhall was to redefine conformity in the 1630s and at the Restoration, they were beyond the pale of the Church of Ireland. Seen from this perspective, Edward Brice was indeed, as Adair claims, the first Presbyterian minister in Ireland. The vertical history of the dissenting churches thus begins in 1634, with the narrowing of the confines of the established church.

But one must not forget the complex reality of the Irish context within which these various groups operated. Edward Brice was also, it must be remembered, collated in 1619 by Bishop Echlin to the prebend of Kilroot in the Church of Ireland, and served that Church in all for twenty-three years, through repeated triennial visitations by an archbishop who had a principled commitment to the distinctive polity of the Church of Ireland. Looked at from this Irish perspective, the pre-history of Irish dissent consists, not of clear lines of descent that can be traced through from the Elizabethan settlement, as in England, but in a broadly based Church of Ireland which, partly through amnesia and carelessness, partly through the principled construction of a tolerant framework, managed the remarkable feat of holding together for two decades the disparate Protestant strands which it had imported from England and Scotland in a peculiarly Irish compromise.

109 NLI, MS 8014/i.

'Into Another Intensity':
Prayer in Irish Nonconformity, 1650–1700

RAYMOND GILLESPIE

Historians who have examined the religion of Irish nonconformists in the later seventeenth century have chosen to approach their subject through its institutional manifestations. There have been a number of studies of individual nonconformist groups from the point of view of their membership. There have also been studies of internal debates over theology and discipline and the usually fractious relations between nonconformist churches and the established church. Yet behind the picture revealed by these studies there lies another problem. The ideas and sources of authority which validated these institutions and which were sufficiently convincing for the laity to submit to their discipline and to contribute financially to their maintenance, have been little studied.

The nonconformist church and its liturgy was shaped and authenticated by its members' experience of God. Those experiences were understood through two sources of Divine inspiration: the revelation of the Bible and the personal revelation of prayer. Prayer was seen as central. As an Independent minister at Limerick in the 1650s, Claudius Gilbert, expressed it, prayer was 'the great engine that moves heaven and earth wherein the meanest may help the greatest' and conversely 'apostacy begins with slight esteem and neglect of prayer, public and private'.[1] From a lay point of view the parliamentary commissioners in the early 1650s stressed that 'we conceive it to be a duty incumbent upon us to mind those that fear the Lord to be frequent in prayer ... And that the Lord renew a spirit of prayer and supplication, a spirit of prevailing with the Lord and of dependence upon Him'.[2] However, prayer was not only about the relationship between God and the petitioner. Such discourse took place in a social context and hence reflected not only ideas about God and the individual but also mirrored the social world in which the prayer was uttered. This essay is an attempt to sketch the outlines of the Irish nonconformist understanding of prayer in the later seventeenth century and to describe some of the social uses to which it was put.

---

1 Claudius Gilbert, *A Pleasant Walk to Heaven* (London, 1658), pp. 49–50.
2 R.M. Young (ed), *Historical Notices of Old Belfast* (Belfast, 1896), p. 112.

I

With the exception of the Quakers, the understanding of prayer by late seventeenth-century nonconformists was that articulated in question 98 of the *Shorter Catechism*, and expanded by its various Irish commentators, such as Thomas Hall and Robert Chambers, Presbyterian ministers at Larne and Dublin respectively. Chambers' himself reflected a number of traditions having gone to the Presbyterians through the established church and, in the 1650s, through the Independents.[3] The picture presented by these men was a fairly orthodox one. Prayer was an offering of the individual's desires to God through the assistance of the Holy Spirit and put up in the name of Christ as the only mediator. Its three forms, petition, confession and thanksgiving, could be offered either as short, 'frequent occasional ejaculations or lifting up of the heart to God', or in longer prayers, 'such as more solemn and stated to keep out distractions'. Such prayers were commanded by God and 'the prayers of the Godly are of great force with God', but yet could not coerce God but rather, 'to confirm our faith we ask what He has promised to give'. Although God had given a form for prayer in the Lord's prayer, man-made forms were frowned on since 'the efficacy of prayer depends more on the holy fervence of affections than the length of words', and that fervency was supplied by the power of the Holy Spirit. The majority of nonconformists stressed order in prayer, a principle they shared with the Church of Ireland. The catechism and the directory of public worship agreed at the Westminster Assembly in 1646 provided the guidelines for prayer. In worship the language of prayer was the vernacular, not the Latin used by Roman Catholics. In public worship it was the clergy who prayed while the congregation gave their assent with 'amen', but at family prayer it was the head of the family who prayed on behalf of all. In theory, although not in practice, the Quaker view of prayer was similar. Within the Quaker assembly anyone might pray either as a representative of the assembly or on behalf of someone else. As with other nonconformists set forms of prayer were prohibited and the work of the Holy Spirit was the main motivator of prayer which was seen as tangible proof of 'the tendering power of the love of God which is ready to attend both young and old'. What upset most nonconformists about early Quaker prayer was its apparent disorder. As Claudius Gilbert put it in 1657, 'they fumed foam, they range and toss ... first ranting, then quaking ... the Ranters were merrily, the Quakers were melancholy mad'.[4]

---

3 Thomas Hall, *A Plain and Easy Explication of the Assembly's Shorter Catechism* (Edinburgh, 1697); Union Theological College, Belfast, MS 'An explanation of the shorter catechism', by Robert Chambers. For Chambers' background, Phil Kilroy, *Protestant Dissent and Controversy in Ireland, 1660–1714* (Cork, 1994), pp. 118–19.
4 Abraham Fuller and Thomas Holme, *A Compendious View of some extraordinary sufferings*

The experience of prayer was shaped by its setting which determined the form and function of the prayer. First there was public prayer in the context of worship which was shaped by a liturgical form such as that contained in the *Directory of Public Worship*. Secondly, families or groups might meet for prayer about common concerns either with or without a minister present. Finally, there was private prayer which touched on yet another range of topics and where the setting might be conducive to meditation as well as vocal prayer. Of these the first was certainly the form most commonly experienced by nonconformists in the later seventeenth century. The *Directory* prescribed that the preaching of the word should be preceded and followed by prayer which was intended to make the preaching more effectual since, in the words of Robert Chambers, 'prayer [was] to bring the effectual blessing of God on both the word and sacrament'. Before the sermon was a prayer of confession which was intended to ensure that the hearers 'be rightly affected with their sins ... and hunger and thirst after the grace of God' about to be revealed. After the sermon was a prayer of thanksgiving and intercession.[5] Such experiences were not confined to Sunday worship. The congregation might gather for prayer on other occasions also, most importantly at times of national or local misfortune when either state, presbytery or congregation might proclaim a fast. The *Directory*, for instance, prescribed that the appropriate response to a judgement of God whether inflicted or imminent was prayer. One Independent minister preaching at Youghal in 1683 told his congregation not to mutter against God in time of trouble 'but lift up your eyes and confess to God, follow him with prayer now in a day of trouble'.[6] Special days of fast and prayer, perhaps because of their very nature, drew more people to church than routine services. At Templepatrick in County Antrim, for example, a normal public collection among the Presbyterian congregation might raise anything between 9*d*. and 1*s*. 10*d*., but a fast day could produce anything from 5*s*. to 9*s*. 2*d*.[7]

No texts of ministerial prayers have survived and hence it is only possible to surmise how such prayers were constructed. The two main influences must have been the *Directory* in terms of content and the Bible for the means of expression. As Robert Chambers explained, 'in church assemblies nothing is to be used but the scriptures and the lively voice of God's own grace in preaching and praying'. Those who could not master these, Chambers claimed,

of the People call'd Quakers (Dublin, 1731), pp. 70, 104, 111; Society of Friends Historical Library, Dublin, MS QM II F1, pp. 61, 68–70; Claudius Gilbert, *The Libertine School'd* (London, 1657), p. 25.

5 *A Confession of Faith* (London, 1859), pp. 365–8, 370–1.

6 National Library of Ireland [hereafter NLI], MS 4201, p. 124.

7 Public Record Office of Northern Ireland [hereafter PRONI], D1759/2B/2, 'Note on public collections, 1688–97'.

should be silenced. In 1659 the Independent Samuel Winter, at a time of political crisis, couched his prayers, following the Bible as a precedent, in imitation of Abraham's intercession for Sodom.[8] Such prayer was intended to be extemporary, although the *Directory* assisted by 'pointing out the heads of those things we are to pray for'. Prayers were composed by the minister and offered by him with the congregation adding only 'amen' at the end to signify their assent. Nonconformists insisted that prayer should not be in an inflexible form but that, since the gift of prayer had been given to everyone, the Holy Spirit should motivate the person praying. William King, bishop of Derry, alleged in the 1690s during his dispute with the Presbyterians over worship that some of them believed 'that all forms of prayer are unlawful for Christians and therefore it is a sin to join in a worship where they are used or to be present at it'.[9] His observation finds some support in the fact that some Presbyterians were prepared to attend Church of Ireland sermons, but would not be present at the reading of prayers.[10]

The lay experience of this type of prayer clearly varied enormously. Some ministers had considerable oratorical skills in prayer. In the 1650s it was said that the prayer of the Independent minister John Murcot of Dublin was 'enlarged, spiritual, powerful to the melting of the congregation unto tears and sighs'.[11] The Presbyterian minister Elias Travers was praised in his funeral sermon at Wood Street by another Presbyterian, Joseph Boyse, who commented that 'his gift of prayer was eminent and edifying. He had a marvellous enlargement of devout affections and copious fluency of suitable scriptural expressions in that heavenly exercise and was thereby happily able to accommodate himself to the various emergent cases of his congregation and of particular persons and families'.[12] While such prayer might, as the catechists maintained, be part of a ministerial calling it was not always dramatic enough to encourage devotion, especially when the congregation had no part in the prayer. While this might be socially undesirable in theological terms it was much more serious in some eyes. At least some nonconformists held that the more people who offered prayer the more effective it would be. In one case at Dublin in 1651 it was claimed that Lieutenant Rogers, a member of John Roger's Independent congregation meeting at Christ Church, had prayed for

8 Chambers, 'An Explanation', pp. 583–8; *The Life and Death of the eminently learned, pious and painful Minister of the Gospel Dr Samuel Winter* (London, 1671), p. 55.

9 William King, *A Discourse concerning the Inventions of Men in the Worship of God* (Dublin, 1694), pp. 43–4.

10 For the attraction of sermons over prayers, Henry Leslie, *A Speech delivered at the Visitation of Down and Connor, held at Lisnegarvey the 26th September 1636* (London, 1639), p. 4; Armagh Public Library, Dopping MSS, no. 36.

11 *Several Works of Mr John Murcot* (London, 1657), p. 21.

12 Joseph Boyse, *The Works of the Learned and Reverend Mr Joseph Boyse of Dublin* (2 vols., London, 1728), i, p. 431.

the safe delivery of his wife, whose pregnancy was difficult, but to no avail. He went to the congregation and asked the assembled saints to pray and she had a safe delivery. Again as Mary Cobb, the sister of the Killileagh Presbyterian James Trail, lay dying in 1715 it was her 'desire to be prayed for in the congregation' as well as prayers at home.[13]

Fortunately aids to devotion were available. For special occasions there were devotional works. Large Presbyterian communions in Ulster, for example, posed particular problems for devotional prayer and here Robert Craghead's manual for communicants proved useful since it offered prayers and meditations for both before and after the reception of the bread and wine.[14] Times of prayer might also be marked off as special by particular postures. As Robert Chambers put it 'we are bound to worship God with our bodies as well as our selves'. There were accepted postures for prayer. For instance, when the Baptist Mary Geale died 'her hands were found in a praying posture'.[15] When praying the normal posture was kneeling. Both Quakers and the Dublin Presbyterians agreed with this and the Independent Thomas Harrison in the 1650s advised of kneeling 'which posture I judge best both for repeating and studying any thing of this nature [prayer]'.[16] Both Quakers and Ulster Presbyterians removed their hats during prayer as they were in the presence of God. The Ulster Presbyterians, unlike their Dublin counterparts refused to kneel during prayer and there the normal practice was to sit. This was a source of embarrassment to the clergy who offered a range of explanations from lack of room to tiredness after a long journey to church, but they agreed the practice was undesirable. At special times, such as the thanksgiving at the communion service, they would stand during prayer.[17]

II

The second form of prayer which the laity might encounter was in the context of the family. Dissenting clergy placed a high premium on this type of prayer. Robert Blair, a Presbyterian minister in County Down in the early seventeenth century, 'prevailed with very many besides their private praying to set up a family prayer in their houses'.[18] In Dublin during the 1650s the

---

13 John Rogers, *Ohel or Beth-shemish* (London, 1653), pp. 369–70; PRONI, D1460/1, f. 20.
14 Robert Craghead, *Advice to Communicants* (Edinburgh, 1659), pp. 82–9.
15 [Ann Fowkes], *A Memoir of Mistress Ann Fowkes (nee Geale)* (Dublin, 1892), p. 13.
16 Thomas Harrison, *Topica Sacra* (London, 1658), p. 172.
17 William King, *A Discourse*, pp. 129–30, 143, 172; Robert Craghead, *An Answer to a Late Book entiled a Discourse concerning the Inventions of Men in the Worship of God* (Edinburgh, 1694), pp. 98–9, 110.
18 Thomas McCrie (ed), *The Life of Mr Robert Blair* (Edinburgh, 1848), p. 63.

Independents likened the family to a 'little church of Jesus Christ' in which prayers were an integral element.[19] How widespread family prayers were is difficult to measure. A number of kirk sessions in County Antrim sent elders to each family to ensure family worship was being observed and in the experience of Joseph Boyse at Dublin dissenting families were five or ten times more likely to have family prayers than those of the Church of Ireland.[20] Family prayer was not entered into lightly. James Trail had little experience of it before his own marriage in 1710. Living with his in-laws he did not establish formal prayers but 'sometime we [himself and his wife] used to join together in prayer to God before he went to bed and by degrees I fell in love with that duty both in secret and with my wife'. When after the birth of his first child he set up his own household 'I began to think it my duty to worship God with my family' and he instituted evening prayer. Two years later he instituted morning prayers as well to ward off the temptations of the day, although few families in his area, except the ministers, had morning prayers.[21]

Family prayer might be supplemented among the godly by meetings of friends for prayer and edifying discussions. Occasionally they might have an evangelical dimension as Edward Wayman in Dublin in the 1650s claimed to have been brought to a conversion experience 'by Mr Fowler and some others and in private meetings and prayers'.[22] Of course meetings for prayer did not have to be this formal. Other settings provided occasions for prayer. Many of the pious on their death beds, for instance, summoned their friends for prayer and to hear their dying speeches but it was in regular prayer meetings that the thinking of the laity on prayer is most clearly displayed.[23] Such meetings can be most clearly seen by examining those associated with the large communion services which were held among the Ulster Presbyterians. John Livingstone, the minister at Killinchy in the 1630s, noted that those attending the communion services 'spent the whole Saturday night in several companies, sometimes a minister being with them, sometimes themselves alone, in conference and prayer'. The practice was carried on through the 1650s and in times when public worship was politically inopportune 'the people would repair to their several societies for prayer the rest of the day, the minister always joining with one of these little societies after another'.[24] Here the presence of

---

19 *The Agreement and Resolution of the Ministers of Christ, Associated within the City of Dublin, and Province of Leinster* (Dublin, 1659), p. 5.
20 PRONI, CR4/12B/1, p. 15; Joseph Boyse, *Remarks on a Late Discourse of William, Lord Bishop of Derry* (London, 1694), p. 64.
21 PRONI, D1460/1, f. 12v–14v.
22 Rogers, *Ohel*, p. 404; PRONI, D1460/1, f. 19v–21v.
23 NLI, MS 4201, pp. 538–9.
24 Thomas Huston (ed), *A Brief History of the Life of Mr John Livingston* (Edinburgh,

the minister was crucial because the societies provided not only opportunities for prayer but also speculation about its nature which was difficult to control given the weak organisational structure of the Ulster Presbyterians at this stage. Thus in the case of a monthly Friday meeting at Oldstone in County Antrim in the 1630s some ministers decided to be present 'to prevent what hurt might follow'.[25] The evidence of what lay speculation might do to ideas about prayer soon became clear. Robert Blair in the 1620s met a man who believed that only prayer was necessary to achieve anything, an idea conceived of his own experience in prayer 'and some other he privately met with'.[26] It was in 1640 that lay ideas of prayer formed in these meetings encountered severe formal disapproval when a number of Irish Presbyterians came into conflict with the General Assembly in Scotland over their style of prayer, one of them describing the Lord's prayer as a 'threadbare prayer'. They opposed all set forms of prayer and objected to private prayers by ministers in church. This, from the General Assembly's point of view, began to resemble Independency and was strongly censured.[27]

For the orthodox, however, the language and themes of lay family or group prayer were influenced by those of the clergy who were held to be most apt at the craft of prayer because of their times of study and private meditation. Some of the more affluent dissenters of an English tradition might maintain domestic chaplains to conduct family worship to an approved standard. Lord Massarene at Antrim maintained a succession of chaplains including John Howe and Elias Travers. At Summerhill in County Meath Mr Tate was domestic chaplain to the Langford family as well as tutor to their children. The earl of Meath supported Daniel Williams in the 1660s and the Countess of Donegal likewise maintained Thomas Emlyn in the 1680s.[28] The conduct and language of prayer was seen as important both in a negative and a positive way. The ability to pray according to the accepted norms was seen as one of the signs of election. Andrew Manwaring, a member of John Roger's Independent Dublin congregation in the 1650s, considered that his personal conversion experience had made him able to pray in the spirit, love the ordinances of the church, and enjoy fellowship with the people of God.[29] From a negative perspective experimentation could have potentially disastrous effects. As the Presbyterian minister at Derry, Robert Craghead, explained:

1848), p. 80; Patrick Adair, *A True Narrative of the Rise and Progress of the Presbyterian Church in Ireland*, W.D. Killen (ed) (Belfast, 1866), p. 183.
25 Adair, *A True Narrative*, p. 321.
26 McCrie, *Life of Blair*, p. 63.
27 W.D. Bailie, *The Sixmilewater Revival of 1625* (Belfast, 1976), pp. 21–2; Marilyn Westerkamp, *The Triumph of the Laity* (Oxford, 1988), pp. 40–1.
28 Kilroy, *Protestant Dissent*, pp. 40–1, 46–7.
29 Rogers, *Ohel*, p. 412 (3).

> If any man use expressions in prayer contrary to the revealed will of
> God and the analogy of faith or such as are not agreeable to the nature
> of prayer or scurilous impertinences such as inevitably rendereth the
> prayer contemptible such a man is so far from praying by the spirit of
> God that where it can be hindered he should not be suffered so to
> profane that holy duty.[30]

Craghead was not alone in voicing such sentiments. James Trail was unwilling
to begin family prayer when he set up his own household in 1710 because he
was afraid that after a few days 'I would be at such a loss for words to express
the sentiments of my mind that I would be obliged to give it over which
would expose me to greater reproach than if I had never began it'. Even when
regular prayer was established in his household he recorded 'the fear I was
under of making some shameful blunder in the performance of it [family
prayer] made me more frequent in my secret address to God for the aid of
His spirit that I might not be put to shame or bring a reproach upon religion
by my misconduct'.[31]

As a result of these concerns the laity drew their family prayers from two
well tested sources. The first was the Bible. The influence here was twofold.
First, the ideas in the text might shape prayer but the Bible might also affect
the language of prayer for Robert Chambers noted, 'it furnishes us with a
variety of meet expressions in prayer'.[32] Certainly the few prayers which were
composed by the Dublin Presbyterian, Dr Duncan Cumyng, were couched in
biblical language with frequent quotations, especially from the Psalms.[33] In
content also the catechisms of Hall and Chambers both stressed that 'some
direction or other may be had from several passages of the holy word of God'
and when praying with the family the head was 'to make more use of scripture and other prayers as helps to prepare him for praying in his family'. The
second inspiration of prayer was the content and language of the sermon.
Sermons might directly contribute to prayer. In 1695 Joseph Boyse observed
that 'words formed into petitions which ministers often in their sermons
suggest to the people when they instruct them in the prayer'.[34] The effect may
have been more indirect. Thomas Harrison, a minister who oscillated between
the Presbyterians and Independents in Dublin, advised that 'every one of you
that would do any good on it to pick out something from every sermon they
hear to be repeated upon their knees in secret'. Robert Craghead agreed
urging that 'it is profitable also on every Lord's day after public worship to

30 Craghead, *An Answer*, p. 51.
31 PRONI, D1460/1, f. 13v–14.
32 Chambers, 'An Explanation', pp. 576.
33 Boyse, *Works*, i, p. 316.
34 Boyse, *Remarks*, p. 32.

meditate what hath been the voice of God to us that day in particular'.[35] In a Baptist family, the Geale household in Kilkenny, the father took down the sermon in shorthand and read it over to his family before prayer.[36] The effect of using these tools might not always be conducive to piety. William King, brought up in a Presbyterian household in the 1650s, later recalled that although there had been family worship every evening led by his father, nevertheless, 'since his prayers were conceived in words and phrases in a manner peculiar to those times and to the sect, I understand them very little and I did not pay much attention to what was done nor could they be easily understood without a dictionary to explain them'.[37]

III

The third form of supplication which nonconformists experienced was personal or private prayer. It is difficult even to suggest the extent to which personal prayer was actually undertaken by the laity. The testimony of King, given before he attended Trinity College, Dublin in 1667, was 'neither had I known nor heard anyone pray to God in secret'. None of his friends at school 'as far as I can remember ... once offered private prayer to God' either night or morning. This he attributed to the abolition of the Book of Common Prayer in the 1650s, so 'it could scarcely happen that rude and illiterate youths could conceive prayers of their own'. Other too were unenthusiastic about prayer and James Trail's servants fell asleep at prayer even though he held it before supper so they would be hungry.[38] However, such experiences should not be considered universal. There are some recorded cases of private prayer which suggest that it was widespread. Praise of 'closet devotions', for example, formed a significant part of Joseph Boyse's funeral sermons for men such as Dr Duncan Cumyng and Arthur Langford.[39] A Kilkenny Baptist, Mary Geale, also prayed alone frequently, her maid noting 'that for a considerable time before her death she used to retire five or six times a day to private prayer'.[40] A crisis might provide the spur to even greater effort in private prayer. John Cook, travelling from Wexford to Kinsale in 1650 spent 16 or 18 hours in private prayer for fear that the ship would sink in a storm.[41]

---

35 Harrison, *Topica Sacra*, p. 172; Craghead, *An Answer*, p. 159.
36 *Memoirs of Ann Fowkes*, p. 33.
37 C.S. King (ed), *A Great Archbishop of Dublin* (London, 1908), p. 10.
38 PRONI, D1460/1, f. 15v; King, *A Great Archbishop*, pp. 9–10.
39 Boyse, *Works*, i, pp. 309, 316.
40 *Memoirs of Ann Fowkes*, pp. 12, 21.
41 *A True Relation of Mr Cooke's Passage by Sea from Wexford to Kinsale* (Cork, 1650), p. 5.

The themes which occupied private prayer can only be surmised. Clearly many were personal and dictated by private priorities. Dr. Cumyng, for instance, prayed for his patients, and Arthur Langford would 'in his audible prayers be much enlarged to begging God [for] the restoration of the oppressed Reformed church abroad and the general enlargement of the interest of the Reformed religion as well as the revival of practical piety in these lands'.[42] Others might be satisfied with less. Joseph Boyse admitted that not everyone had the gift of prayer, 'and therefore they often urge such to the use of forms'. Although this was not encouraged, even the austere Robert Craghead was prepared to concede that 'as for the young and very ignorant people we allow them the use of forms until God enable them more'.[43] The form might be the Lord's prayer although in the diocese of Derry William King alleged that 'a great many' of the Presbyterians did not know the Lord's prayer.[44] There was a via media between entirely inspired prayer and the use of a form. This was the use of prayer manuals which while not providing the words for prayer suggested themes or guidelines for the advance composition of prayers by the devout. Both of these techniques were used in late seventeenth-century Ireland. In the 1650s, for example, a primer existed in Ireland containing prayers for Oliver Cromwell as Lord Protector, but it was banned in 1662.[45] Thomas Harrison, Independent minister at Christ Church in succession to John Rogers, had more success with his prayer manual *Topica Sacra* published in 1658 which was based on a series of sermons in Christ Church. This provided a series of prayer themes in the form of argument with God for 'the blessed work of pleading and striving and wrestling with God'. There were themes for prayers, for example, in case of fear of spiritual judgement, intercessions for others, in case of pain, for fear of unbelief, for fear of affliction. All were strongly influenced by biblical themes and biblical language predominated.

An alternative to using books of prayers was to compile one's own. Joseph Boyse, for instance, was not prepared to exclude premeditation as to the words of prayers as a valid way of praying.[46] A number of Dublin Presbyterians did compose such prayers. Anne Reading of Rathfarnham wrote prayers and meditations throughout her life. Dr Cumyng composed prayers for use on various occasions but to prevent these from becoming mere forms 'he strictly observed what returns were made to them'.[47] James Trail also thought

---

42 Boyse, *Works*, i, pp. 309.
43 Craghead, *An Answer*, p. 62; Boyse, *Remarks*, p. 53.
44 William King, *An Admonition to the Dissenting Inhabitants of the Diocese of Derry* (Dublin, 1694), pp. 5–6, 23.
45 Richard Mant, *A History of the Church of Ireland from the Reformation to the Revolution* (London, 1840), p. 634.
46 Boyse, *Remarks*, p. 55.
47 Boyse, *Works*, i, pp. 173, 316.

a good deal about his prayers before worship, rising early in the morning for 'reading and meditating for subject matter for petition and thanksgiving' as well as examining himself in which 'I found out much guilt'.[48]

It was through private prayer that the heights and depths of spiritual experience were plumbed. For some, private prayer had little effect. Thomas Smith, the Quaker linen weaver from Chapelizod confessed in 1692 that he had heard God's voice calling him and had gone to a private place to pray but did not recognise the voice of God until his convincement as a Quaker.[49] In the 1650s Humphrey Mills in Dublin had a more traumatic experience for he 'wept often and bitterly and prayed earnestly but yet had no comfort'.[50] Many were, however, affected deeply. The young James Trail, not noted for the piety which characterised his later life, prayed after a number of disputes with his brother so that:

> I did sometimes with an abundance of tears confess and bewail my conduct before God and to beg of Him to subdue my violent passions ... though I must confess my heart was so deeply and tenderly affected in my acknowledgement before God on these occasions it made an impression on my mind that when I think of it to this day the idea how I was then affected often returns to my mind and I have often since endeavoured to draw some comfort from it.[51]

For others private prayers had yet more dramatic effects. Elizabeth Avery, a member in Dublin of John Rogers' independent congregation during the 1650s, recounted her conversion experience to the congregation, 'as I was at prayer God wonderfully appeared and then it was that Christ was manifested to my spirit and I was in a trance for a while but after I awakened full of joy'. Jeremy Hayward of the same congregation on a Sunday 'fell into prayer, I prayed thrice and at the third time I heard Him say "Lo! My grace is sufficient for thee" whereby I was much satisfied ever since'.[52] Prayer was not confined to conversion experiences. The Kilkenny Baptist, Ann Fowkes, noted that private prayer 'became not only familiar but delightful', and

> I have been so carried out at the sacrament and private prayer that I have ardently wished for wings as a dove that I might fly away and so be at rest. Blessed be God I have since often known, but especially then, what it was to have my heart burn within me whilst my belov'd and my God was present in this ordinance.[53]

---

48 PRONI, D1460/1, f. 14–14v.
49 Society of Friends Historical Library, Dublin, MS MM II F1, p. 165.
50 Rogers, *Ohel*, pp. 407, 410.
51 PRONI, D1460/1, f. 4.
52 Rogers, *Ohel*, pp. 404, 415.   53 *Memoir of Mistress Ann Fowkes*, pp. 44, 47.

IV

The experience of God in the varying types of prayers which nonconformists practised and encouraged confirmed them in one important belief, that prayer gave them direct access to the power of God. In removing relics and other intermediate ways of gaining access to God nonconformist groups exalted vocal and mental prayer and transferred functions to it which in traditional Catholic practice had been performed in other ways by, for example, pilgrimage or relics. Admittedly access throught prayer to God was conditional. Theologians taught that one could not pray for everything. Those who commented on the catechism stressed this point. Thomas Hall glossed question 98 of the shorter catechism that we may only petition for good things, agreeable to God's will, and pray against evil things. Thomas Chambers, commenting on question 99, explained that these included covetousness, distrust of providence and discontentment with one's condition. In 1714 Joseph Boyse expressed it in a sermon,

> the less we have of any private views or particular interests in our eye and the more we have of the advancement of God's honour and interest and the real welfare of sacred and civil society at heart the more our prayers are conformed to the will of God and consequently entitled to a gracious audience from Him.[54]

It followed from this that one could not compel God to do anything. To turn a request into a charm which would be a guarantee was sinful and popish. To use 'charms, figures, sorceries etc' was a great sin according to Robert Chambers. He also showed how in the case of the Lord's prayer 'papists make a charm of it and the poor and ignorant people rest in the repetition of the bare words'. But as Robert Craghead pointed out the efficacy of prayer was not in the words for that was a popish doctrine.[55] However such distinctions made by theologians were too abstruse for some of the laity who persisted in seeing prayer as a way of accessing the power of God to achieve particular ends. Robert Blair, the Presbyterian minister in County Down, consulted one of his flock about a sick horse in 1624. He was told 'there was need of no other means to be used but prayer whatever ailed soul or body, young or old, corn or cattle ... I need not use any other help but to go to my chamber and pray for him [the horse]'. The wife of Colonel Jones of Kilkenny adopted a similar position when she fell ill in the 1650s for after she had been prayed for she

---

54 *The Life and Death ... of Samuel Winter*, pp. 48–9; Boyse, *Works*, i, p. 374.
55 Boyse, *Remarks*, p. 32; Craghead, *An Answer*, p. 37; Chambers, 'An Explanation', p. 666.

refused medicine 'for she would not dishonour God and wrong prayer so much'.[56]

This understanding of prayer as a way of accessing the power of God made it more than a devotional tool. It became a strategy for tackling a wide range of problems. Troubled with recalcitrant tenants in 1713 James Trail 'waited upon God by prayer for some time for light and direction how to manage it'.[57] Treatment provided by the Presbyterian Dr Duncan Cumyng in Dublin meant more than just medical advice since 'he followed his advice to his endangered patients with earnest requests for the Divine blessing in order to [aid] their recovery'.[58] The same theme was echoed by the Independent Samuel Winter who, preaching in Dublin in the 1650s, defined prayer as 'an ordinance to which God hath made such a gracious promise and he often doth restore the sick [through] prayers being put up for them'. Winter himself had considerable success in curing people by prayer including his nephew, sister-in-law and the wife of Colonel Jones of Kilkenny.[59] As disorders moved away from the purely physical ailment so the importance of the supernatural in explaining the causes and the power of prayer to counteract them increased. At the simplest this might involve behaviour which could be explained as the temptations of the world which required prayer to counteract them. Thus in the 1660s when the husband of the Kilkenny Baptist, Mary Geale, took to 'keeping company' with idle companions in a public house she began to 'pray for him. Jacob-like she wrestled with God and prevailed for it pleased the Lord to let him see his folly and he became a sober man'.[60]

Not all cases were so simple. Anti-social behaviour could shade into the murkier worlds of witchcraft and demon possession. Nonconformists did not deny the reality of these experiences. As Revd James Alexander, the Presbyterian minister of Convoy in County Donegal, put it in a sermon of August 1685 'the devils indwelling in a man's body, a thing frequent in our Lord's day and not so rare now a days as we imagine'. Robert Chambers explained signs of evil as the possession of bodies 'by witchcraft possession'.[61] Traditional Catholic practice had a range of devices for dealing with these problems, from exorcism by the clergy to the protective powers of relics, but these were concentrated into prayer by nonconformists. In the battle against the diabolic, supernatural prayer was the chief weapon. In 1678, for example, a

---

56 McCrie, *Life of Blair*, p. 63; *The Life and Death ... of Samuel Winter*, p. 46.

57 PRONI, D1460/1, f. 16v.

58 Boyse, *Works*, i, p. 316.

59 Samuel Winter, *The Summe of Diverse Sermons* (Dublin, 1656), p. 105; *The Life and Death ... of Samuel Winter*, pp. 43–6, 50, 53–5.

60 *Memoirs of Mistress Ann Fowkes*, p. 8.

61 Presbyterian Historical Society, Belfast, Sermons of Revd James Alexander of Convoy, 1672–86; Chambers, 'An Explanation', p. 663.

Dublin house haunted by mysterious noises was exorcised by the Presbyterian minister Daniel Williams and some of his colleagues. They spent a night in prayer in the house and concluded with a sermon on Hebrews 2: 18.[62] Robert Blair was faced with a more dramatic situation in 1624 when he was faced with a man who claimed that the devil had ordered him to kill Blair. As at Dublin the successful exorcism began with prayer, then a sermon and further prayers followed by 'intermixing of prayer and singing until morning'.[63] In 1710 another Presbyterian minister, Mr Sinclair, had less effect in a witchcraft case at Islandmagee. A woman, Mary Dunbar, was 'much afflicted' by local witches who tormented her when Sinclair prayed with her 'and told her they would hinder her of hearing his prayers'.[64] This sort of exorcist activity was usually confined to the clergy but not always. When it was revealed in 1672 that the Revd James Shaw of Carnmoney had been bewitched by his servant, George Russell, who had called up a spirit, the Antrim meeting ordered Russell to 'study knowledge and pray' to counteract the spirit and when this failed to work they ordered a fast.[65] Again in Dublin during the 1650s the Baptist, Heirome Sankey attempted an exorcism on Mr Wadman which failed. He concluded that 'Wadman's devil was of the sort that required fasting as well as prayer to expel it'.[66]

The understanding of prayer as an access to the divine was so important to nonconformists in the later seventeenth century that its use could not be limited to the roles of healing. In a world where transcendence and immanence were indissoluble, supernatural power had an important role to play in validating the correctness of political or religious positions. Central to this was the doctrine of providence through which God manifested his approbation of the actions of one particular individual or group. The Calvinist branches of nonconformity with their doctrine of the elect and the ecclesiology of the gathered saints emphasised this yet further. A Dublin Independent, Samuel Mather, noted in the 1660s 'there is no scruple made of joining together as prayer and preaching and hearing one another which is ordinarily practised in this city'.[67] Practices of prayer also divided. The Church of Ireland tradition of set forms and a wider congregational role in liturgical prayers (or as Samuel Mather described it 'absurd broken responses and tossing of their prayers like tennis balls') ensured that there could be little common ground between the two groups and was deemed to confirm the election of particular congrega-

62 Richard Baxter, *The Certainty of the World of Spirits* (London, 1691), pp. 218–19.
63 McCrie, *Life of Blair*, p. 68.
64 Young, *Old Belfast*, pp. 161–2.
65 PRONI, D1759/1A/2, pp. 54, 57.
66 *Reflections on Some Persons and Things in Ireland by Letters sent to and from Dr Petty* (London, 1660), pp. 101–2.
67 Samuel Mather, *Irenicum; or An Essay for Union* (London, 1680), p. 2.

tions.[68] The prayers of the godly in a godly cause, as mediated by the saints, could not fail to be answered. As the Ulster Presbyterian, Robert Craghead, explained in his debate with Bishop King on worship, 'yet truth being on our side and he [King] being the first aggressor there is no fear but the God of truth will thoroughly plead his own cause'.[69] The point was nicely made in 1670 when the Presbyterians of Ulster called a fast because of poor weather which threatened the harvest. Patrick Adair noted that 'the Lord visibly answered prayer by a remarkable change of seasons immediately after' and those who were not Presbyterians 'thanked God—since none would pray— that the presbyterians prayed and fasted and had obtained rain and a good season'.[70]

In this case prayer defined the nonconformist groupings against others and ensured that prayer for themselves, and more importantly against their enemies, conformed to the ideas of the catechism that one should only pray for things agreeable to God's will. Their asking for God's blessing on their friends and political loyalties, for the most part, ensured that prayers for the king as head of state were an important part of liturgical prayer. Those, such as the Ulster covenanters who followed Jeremiah Marsden at Dublin in the 1660s, who omitted to pray for the king were severely censured.[71] It was appropriate that before the abortive rising of Colonel Thomas Blood in 1663 the plotters and their supporters 'had three meetings the day before at three separate places to seek the Lord for a blessing'.[72] Prayer became a dramatic way of dealing with opponents. When George Wild, bishop of Derry, tried to break up a Presbyterian meeting in 1661 he was 'boldly reviled by their hot spirited women who told him they would pray him to distraction'.[73] Wild was not the only bishop to suffer in this way. In 1695 William King claimed that some Presbyterian ministers in Derry 'do pray against me in their pulpits'.[74] This was not a new practice. During the 1650s it was complained that in Cork some ministers used 'some unbecoming prayers against the state' and at Broadisland in County Antrim it was reported to the council at Dublin in 1652 that the Presbyterian minister 'hath been observed to use a passage in his prayer to this effect "Lord wilt thou be pleased to give the whip into our hands again and Thou shall see how we will scourge the enemies of Thy people". '[75]

68 Samuel Mather, *The Figures or Types of the Old Testament* (Dublin, 1683), p. 361.
69 Craghead, *An Answer*, sig A2v.
70 Adair, *A True Narrative*, pp. 294–5.
71 Kilroy, *Protestant Dissent*, pp. 294–5.
72 *Calendar of State Papers Relating to Ireland, 1663–5*, p. 133.
73 NLI, MS 8643 (1).
74 William King, *A Second Admonition to the Dissenting Inhabitants of the Diocese of Derry* (Dublin, 1695), p. 29.
75 National Archives, Dublin, M2817, p. 50; Young, *Historical Notices*, p. 76.

Using prayer in this way as a request for supernatural validation for a particular political or theological position was fraught with dangers. Not the least of these was that if the prayer was unanswered it called into question the very basis of the existence of the gathered saints. Both clergy and laity therefore took the problem of unanswered prayer seriously. The clergy refused to acknowledge that God might not answer prayer. Instead they stressed the different ways in which prayer might be answered. Thomas Harrison argued that 'arguments then in prayer are not likely to go unanswered and praying souls find it so. Sometimes He answers gloriously ... sometimes He answers in some secret support only ... sometimes God answers in some providential dispensation which doth gratify us for the present and might instruct us for the future' but he did note that the language of prophecy was difficult to interpret.[76] In 1668 at Dublin the Independent Samuel Mather took up the same theme in a sermon. Here he stressed the difficulty of understanding the mind of God in answering prayer for 'God answers the prayers of His people sometimes by wonderful and terrible things in Righteousness as in Psalm 65: 5. The most dreadful revelations of providence are in answer to prayer'. In a later sermon reflecting on chapters eight and nine of Revelation in which prayer brought not blessing but adversity and 'the strange power of God did answer the prayers of His people this way. It is the prayers of God's people that turns the whole of providence as it were and brings about all the great and mighty revolutions in the course thereof'.[77] As Jeremy Taylor, bishop of Down and Connor, reported at a time of reversal of Presbyterian hopes for toleration in 1660 their ministers prayed 'that the Lord though He suffers these wolves, the bishops, to come unto this kirk on earth yet that He would never let them come into his kirk in heaven'.[78]

Almost by definition prayer by a member of the elect could not go unanswered but the form of the answer was not necessarily the anticipated one. At least some were not convinced by this argument and developed another. Dr Cumyng, according to Joseph Boyse in his funeral sermon in 1724, noted his prayers:

> [He] strictly observed what returns were made to them. And though he made frequent complaints to God of his prayers being (as he thought) unheard and unanswered under the many afflictive trials he met with yet he still justified God, condemned himself, expressed a reverential subjection to the will of God, the resolution still to call on Him, often

76 Harrison, *Topica Sacra*, pp. 13–15.
77 Mather, *Figures or Types of the Old Testament*, pp. 320, 508.
78 Bodleian Library, Oxford, Carte MS 45, f. 29.

adopting the words of the pious Job 'Though He stay me yet will I have trust in Him'.[79]

Traces of this explanation can also be found in Thomas Harrison's *Topica sacra* which relied heavily on the books of Job and Jeremiah for biblical references for its prayer themes. Thus prayer by its very nature as a channel to the supernatural could not fail and so provided validation for the existence of nonconformity in the later seventeenth century.

V

In attempting to understand the working of nonconformity in seventeenth century Ireland, prayer must be assigned a major role in describing religiosity. Prayer in various forms provided a direct access to God. For many this experience was probably restricted to a weekly religious service, but for others it was also a daily practice either as part of a family group or privately. For the godly the experience of private prayer was the continuation of their conversion experience. For others prayer had a more practical role as curer of physical or supernatural ills and definer and validator of the entire nonconformist structure. However nonconformity is viewed, prayer lies at its core.

79 Boyse, *Works*, i, p. 316.

'A Gay and Flattering World': Irish Baptist Piety and Perspective, 1650–1780

KEVIN HERLIHY

The piety and perspective of the Irish Baptists evolved through various stages which were closely connected to optimism and pessimism. Early on their theology and perspective can be broadly categorised as optimistic. However, by the mid-eighteenth century their general religious thought patterns had become overwhelmingly pessimistic. These stages did not follow neat patterns whereby hopefulness was clearly replaced by doubt, but rather there was a continual flow away from a confident view. Their retreat began early in the second half of the seventeenth century. When Baptist ideas were first promulgated on a large scale in England during the early 1640s, many of their evangelists possessed a lively theology and perspective that was attractive and appealing to many in their audience. However, early in the 1650s traces of ideological faltering were becoming apparent in the thought of English Baptist leaders. In Ireland doubt and suspicion entered into the Baptist frame of mind somewhat later in the decade and became even more marked after the Restoration. At the turn of the eighteenth century the residual confidence of the founding members from the Cromwellian period was fading as quickly as that generation was passing. But the financial resources of that generation did induce a slight resurgence of aplomb within the Irish Baptist community, albeit a short-lived one. By the later half of the eighteenth century self-doubt and suspicion of others had become a predominant part of their piety and perspective. This essay is primarily concerned with how this transformation came to pass.

I

English Baptists from their beginning were a people who distrusted hierarchical ecclesiastical power. In 1641 the London merchant and pastor William Kiffin, the most prominent and politically influential seventeenth-century Baptist, stated his view on ecclesiastical power by saying, 'Christ hath not given this power to his church, not to a hierarchy, neither to a national presbytery, but to a company of saints in a congregational way'. In other words, he believed that the power of the church should be dispersed and spread among individual churches or meetings. Church sovereignty was to rest in the local congregation. The local congregation was to be made up of believing individuals meeting in voluntary association which in turn formed affiliations with other like-minded congregations.[1] Rather than a presbytery or synod Baptists chose a form of church polity that fitted in with their ecclesiastical ideals and called it an 'Association'. The emphasis placed on church government was that of liberality, reflecting their self-confidence and optimism.

At this stage liberal ideas played an important part in their polemic. In 1644 Christopher Blackwood, who later became a well-known preacher in the early Irish community, wrote an exposition on freedom of speech and conscience. In that treatise he argued quite strenuously for toleration of diverse religious ideas that were being put forth by hitherto repressed preachers. According to Blackwood 'Anti-Christ', working through a hierarchical ecclesiastical and political structure, was the only one interested in confining the preaching of the godly. He certainly thought that unrestricted preaching would risk a certain amount of 'chaos', but the risk was worthwhile because he innocently believed that the process of spiritual regeneration would eventually lead to a 'thorow' reformation of society. Repression, however, might cause society to lose the benefit of potential reformers analogous to Martin Luther or John Calvin.[2]

In addition to their liberality many Baptists in England rejoiced in the general breakdown of authority as a result of the English civil wars. For instance, Captain Richard Lawrence, who later became a colonel in Ireland, applauded the emergence of so-called 'mechanic preachers' in the 1640s.[3] These preachers, many of whom were Baptists or at least rejected infant baptism, were theologically untrained men from the lower socio-economic strata. Some had been 'soap boylers' and 'water carriers' before they took up preaching. They also exhorted people with an unconventional theology that many times was seen as socially dangerous and seditious by champions of the status quo.[4] Many of higher social rank, who had supported the English

1 W[illiam] K[iffin], A Glimpse of Sion's Glory (London, 1641).
2 Christopher Blackwood, The Storming of Anti-christ; Compulsion of Conscience his last Garrison (London, 1644), pp. 4–14.
3 Richard Lawrence, The Wolf Stript of his Sheeps Clothing, or The Antichristian Clergyman turn'd right side outwards (London, 1647), pp. 6, 20–1.
4 Thomas Edward, Gangraena: or A Catalogue and Discovery of many of the Errours, Heresies, Blasphemies and pernicious Practices of the Sectaries of this time vented and acted in England in these four last years ([facs. ed. by The Rota] London, 1646), epistle dedicatory; A.L. Morton, The World of the Ranters: Religious Radicalism in the English Revolution (London, 1970), pp. 20–35; Murray Tolmie, The Triumph of the Saints; the London Separate Churches, 1609–1649 (Cambridge, 1977), p. 31.

parliamentary cause, found the religious expression of the lower orders threatening. In 1659 the London Presbyterian pastor Richard Baxter, looking back on the 1640s, claimed that the 'Old Cause' that Parliament had fought for was 'the Rights and Liberties of the People, and not their Soveraignty'. Baxter thought that it was a clear precept that the 'ignorant rabble' had to be suppressed by an educated and godly elite.[5] Baptists, on the contrary, were able to make successful appeals to the lower orders. In 1647 Lawrence published two short tracts attacking clerical power. One was aimed at clerics in general and another was aimed specifically at Presbyterian clerics. At this time Lawrence was laudatory in claiming that the emergence of mechanic preachers had taken place 'especially these five or six last years, since their persecutors have had no leasure (sic) to look after them'. He looked to Scripture texts which affirmed God's favour for the lower orders and resistance to the high-born. Although the saints were still a minority this was no impediment to confidence. After all, Lawrence was able to cite passages in the Bible that clearly showed the godly in adversarial situations which they were able to overcome.[6] This type of sentiment was expressed most radically in the ideology of the Levellers, and later in the anti-aristocratic rhetoric of the Fifth Monarchy Men. Although many Baptist leaders refrained from levelling they did, like Lawrence, have views that were disparaging of social rank. In June 1653 Baptists in Ireland sent a letter to their co-religionists in England and Wales claiming that God's 'hand hath byn still streached forth to sett his poore dispised ones on high from the kings of the earth'. They further claimed that God had 'cast contempt uppon princes' and 'greatly reproved kings and mighty men'.[7] These representations are very understandable because many initial recruits to the Baptist cause were from the 'lower and middling sort', and were enthusiastic supporters of the English Parliament in its victory over the Royalists.

Another example of this liberal attitude can be seen in John Vernon, who served in the 1650s as a captain in the Cromwellian army in Ireland. In 1648 he had published a pamphlet advocating the end of all civil authority over religious activities. He appealed to the 'Parable of the Tares' (Matthew 13: 24–30, Mark 4: 26–9) for proof:

---

5 Richard Baxter, *The Holy Commonwealth* (London, 1659), addition to the preface, pp. 92–4, 226–9; C. Hill, *The World Turned Upside Down* (London, 1972), pp. 32ff.
6 Richard Lawrence, *The Antichristian Presbyter, or Antichrist Transformed: Assuming the New Shape of a Reformed Presbyter, as His Last and Sublest Disquise to Deceive the Nations* (London, 1647); idem, *The Wolf Stript*, p. 7.
7 Swanzey Baptist Church, Swanzey, Massachusetts, Ilston Church Book, pp. 80–2; National Library of Wales, Aberystwyth, Deposit 409B, Llanwenarth Church Book, pp. 11–12. Also printed, B.R. White (ed), *Association Records of the Particular Baptists of England, Wales and Ireland to 1660, Part 2* (London, 1974), pp. 111–24.

that men, though the servants of Christ, and clearly discerning his Enemies, may not yet pluck them up, or restrain them by Humane Power without trespass, against the express command of Christ, who hath reserved that work to his Harvest, the end of the world.[8]

The authority of the magistrate was to be replaced by countering religious opposition with 'Peace, Love, Gentleness, glad Tidings, Freedom, and not forcible restraint'.[9] Surely self-interest prompted such an idea because Baptist preachers and pastors had been the targets of civil repression. Vernon also expressed a levelling predilection. In March 1654 while he was serving in Ireland he wrote to Oliver Cromwell and explained the downfall of Charles I. The king had fallen because he and his party 'walked in pride' with a strength that was based on 'Magisty proved weake'. The 'upright ones' who 'being then few & not many wise nor skillfull' had been victorious because of God's adjudication.[10] Nevertheless his ideas and arguments, like Blackwood and Lawrence, placed a great emphasis on liberty of conscience for the godly.

Religious chaos ensued during the 1640s as a result of wide-spread theological speculation among the literate and semi-literate. Many questioned and rejected the fundamental assumptions of the Protestant Reformation and were not so much interested in reform as in starting over anew with a unique set of assumptions. Such speculation eventually led many to desire a more 'thorow' reformation than most Baptist leaders were willing to accept. Vehement attacks denouncing the clergy as deceivers and seducers led some, like the Digger leader Gerrard Winstanley, to reject any form of ecclesiastical organisation. Other religious radicals, like the Seekers, abandoned clerical authority on the basis of a belief that the 'Truth' had been lost and therefore no one was able to claim spiritual authority. The Quakers emerged following this vein of thought. They were motivated by an eschatological belief that the age of the 'spirit' was dawning and that salaried clergy and sacraments were no longer binding. Although Baptist leaders shared the primary radical impulse of Diggers, Seekers and Quakers their leaders never really questioned the underlying basis of Protestant thought at that time: the Bible. Another motivating factor in not following through with the radical impulse was their opposition's criticism. Baptists were constantly reminded that those who preached and practised believer's baptism in sixteenth-century Germany brought with them social cataclysm.[11]

8 John Vernon, *The Sword's Abuse Asserted: or, A Word to the Army* (n.p., 1648), p. 4
9 Ibid., p. 7.
10 British Library, London, Add. MS 4166, ff. 49–50.
11 Christopher Hill, *The World Turned Upside Down* (London, 1972); Morton, *The World of the Ranters*, pp. 20–35; J.F. McGregor, 'The Baptists: Fount of All Heresy' in Barry Reay and J.F. McGregor (eds), *Radical Religion in the English Revolution* (Oxford, 1986), p. 26.

So in a very short time experience and polemic had altered Baptist confidence in emancipation. After the Presbyterians were purged from the English Parliament and Charles I was executed Baptist leaders in London began to fear excesses. In 1650 the London Baptists published a pamphlet entitled *Heart-Bleedings for Professors Abominations*. The epistle utilised the earliest Christian creed, the *Apostle's* Creed. The motivation for this public appeal was two-fold. Baptists were often acridly and wrongly accused of libertine practices by religious opponents. Therefore they did not want to be associated with supporting or defending morally repugnant behaviour of which they themselves did not approve. However, at this time they were still advocating religious liberty based on toleration of belief, if not behaviour. The target of their moral attack was not any specific sect, but rather Antinomian doctrine— those who taught that believers need not obey religious morality laws. They declared unambiguously their revulsion at some perceived excesses by stating emphatically that some Antinomian practices were 'against civil societies, violating the bonds of marriage, and Laws of families'. Even heathen societies did not behave this way, therefore, the licentious 'justly incur the punishment of the rulers of this world'. It was very natural for Baptist leaders to change tack because, after supporting the victors in the civil wars, many now enjoyed wealth and prestige and the political power and influence that went with it. Therefore, these leaders wanted to cultivate an image of respectability for the view of the wider world in which they lived.[12]

During the 1640s and beyond Baptists were buffeted from without and within leading to a revision of their rudimentary notions. Many contemporaries believed that their rejection of infant baptism placed the institution of marriage in jeopardy. Perceptions of Baptists were also shaped by the high level of infant mortality in the seventeenth century and the consequent anxiety concerning the spiritual status of infants. Propaganda against Baptists exploited this disquietude. One pamphlet in 1645 made the audacious claim that a woman in Dover had beheaded her own baby to prevent its being baptised.[13] The mode of baptism practised by Baptists was immersion in water, usually in a river at night. This caused trepidation, suspicion and ridicule among outsiders. In 1645 an anti-Baptist tract featured on the cover naked women in a river about to be baptised and sarcastically labelled them 'Virgins of Sion'.[14] As a result of outside pressure it was only natural that the Baptist leadership would want to present a scandal-free image to the outside world. The London Baptists were leading the way in establishing rules of

12 [John Spilsbury], *Heart-Bleedings for Professors Abominations* (London, 1650); M. Tolmie, *The Triumph of the Saints*, chapter eight.
13 *Strange News from Kent* (London, 1645).
14 Daniel Featley, *The Dippers Dipt* (London, 1645), title page. The drawing is also reproduced on the cover of Tolmie, *The Triumph of the Saints*.

conduct for their members because there were many who had speculated their way past baptism in the 1640s before moving on to more radical beliefs. Sometimes these individuals who had already passed were still thought of by critics as Baptists. Therefore it was incumbent on their leaders to establish stability in their church communities to assuage the fears of the extraneous.[15]

II

Many Baptist personalities who were part of the army that came to Ireland in the early 1650s held important military, ministerial or civilian positions in the Cromwellian establishment. Among these were at least seven military governors at one time or another in the early 1650s; Colonels Richard Lawrence, William Leigh and Richard Le Hunt in Waterford; Colonel Daniel Axtell in Kilkenny; Colonel Heirom Sankey in Clonmel; Major John Nelson was commander-in-chief at Kerry; and Lieutenant Paul Dod at Galway.[16] There were numerous other men of high military rank. Baptists also held important ministerial posts. Thomas Patient was preacher to the army officers and the Lord Deputy, Charles Fleetwood. Christopher Blackwood's stipend of £200 per annum indicates that his ministerial post was distinguished. In addition there were at least eight other Baptist ministers on the civil list in the early 1650s.[17] In Dublin there were Baptists of high status serving in civilian capacities; Dr Philip Carteret was an attorney serving as Advocate General; James Standish was Deputy Treasurer; and Edward Roberts was Auditor General.[18] In October 1655 Thomas Harrison reported to the Secretary of State, John Thurloe, on the state of the 'Anabaptists' in Ireland:

> alas how is this land shared out amongst persons of this perswasion, governors of towns and cities 12 at least, collonells 10, lieut. colonels 3

15 An example of someone moving on from Baptists ideas to more radical ideas is Laurence Clarkson. His career is discussed in A.L. Morton, *The World of the Ranters*, pp. 123–42.

16 Kevin Herlihy, 'The Irish Baptists, 1650–1780' PhD thesis, Trinity College, Dublin (1992), appendix i; R. Dunlop (ed), *Ireland Under the Commonwealth* (2 vols., Manchester, 1913), i, pp. 29n, 395–6, ii, pp. 711n; White, *Association Records*, pp. 120, 124n; Ilston Church Book, pp. 80–2; Llanwenarth Church Book, pp. 11–12; J. Nicholls (ed), *Original Letters and Papers of State Addressed to Oliver Cromwell* (London, 1743), p. 149.

17 St. John Seymour, *The Puritans in Ireland* (Oxford, 1919), pp. 206–24; Bodleian Library, Oxford, Rawlinson MS A208, pp. 379, 390, 410, 421, 427; Cited in T.C. Barnard, *Cromwellian Ireland* (Oxford, 1975) p. 102n.

18 Rawlinson MS A13, f. 25; T. Birch (ed) *A Collection of the State Papers of John Thurloe* (7 vols., London, 1742), iii, 445; Dunlop, *Ireland under the Commonwealth*, i, p. 324.

or 4, majors 10, captains 19 or 20, preachers in salary 2, officers in the civil list 23, and many of whome I never heard.[19]

His estimation of Baptist strength was exaggerated when considering that the size of the army was 35,000 in at least 300 garrisons.[20] Also, it is not clear whether or not Harrison was using the epithet 'Anabaptist' loosely. The temptation was very great to tar anyone with unorthodox or radical religious opinions as an Anabaptist. However, it is very clear that initially Baptists held positions of respect and esteem in Cromwellian Ireland which no doubt inspired confidence.

In the early 1650s Baptists along with other religious and political radicals in Ireland were at their zenith both politically and numerically. They were part of an army with a long record of victory and the Lord Deputy of Ireland, Charles Fleetwood, was well-disposed toward them. However, political rivalry between army leaders and 'Ancient Protestants' (pre-Cromwellian Protestants) led to Fleetwood being replaced and their subsequent political demotion. Unfortunately for the Baptists many important non-Baptist personalities who supported them also had their power reduced when Henry Cromwell assumed complete authority of Ireland in September 1655. Due to the heavy tax burden it was necessary for the regime to disband the army and return political authority to civilian rule. It was at this time that Baptists and their Separatist allies in the army were forced to relinquish power in a mild political struggle that lasted until December 1656.[21] At this time the adjutant-general, Captain William Allen, made the astute observation that 'when the people of God are in prosperity knights would frequent their meetings'.[22] For many, the chief motivation for becoming affiliated with the Baptists and other political and religious radicals was the hope of personal advancement through endorsements by politically proficient members. Therefore their loss of political prestige resulted in a trimming of their support. Some members left the Baptist fold because they sought better political and economic opportunities in Ireland, still others, while remaining in the fold, sought better political advantages in England. Axtell, Allen and Vernon were less willing to make political compromises and left Ireland in the summer of 1657. They returned to England in search of increased political power and to oppose the policies of the regime.[23]

19 *Thurloe State Papers*, iv, pp. 90–1.
20 National Library of Wales, Letterbook of Col John Jones, MS 11,440D, p. 62; Rawlinson MS A16, p. 1.
21 Herlihy, 'Irish Baptists', chapter two; Barnard, *Cromwellian Ireland*, pp. 98–109.
22 *Thurloe State Papers*, iv, p. 327.
23 Ibid., p. 729; William Allen, *A Relation of the Release of Mrs. Huish from under the Tempter* (London, 1658), preface; idem, *A Faithful Memorial of the Remarkable Meet-*

Because Henry Cromwell's 'inclination' was 'not to crush them quite' some Baptist leaders in Ireland were able to retain positions of prominence and prestige.[24] In the late 1650s those Baptists who remained in Ireland, by and large, adapted very well. In 1657 Richard Lawrence published *Gospel Separation Separated from its Abuses* whereby he argued for the godly to be moderate toward one another. He feared the 'saints' or the 'godly party' was losing its influence on society. His conciliatory and temperate tone was generally reciprocated by his fellow Protestants. The following year a group of ministers from Dublin and the rest of Leinster met to devise a theological formulation based on compromise. The result was *The Agreement and Resolution of the Ministers of Christ*. While affirming the propriety of infant baptism and condemning a variety of doctrinal errors they did not single out the Baptists, or even believer's baptism, for doctrinal censure. The Protestant community was relatively small and the prominent personalities within it were well-known to one another.[25]

Even though in the late 1650s some of their opponents were printing propaganda disparaging them as ranters, crackpots and associating them with the old story of religious chaos at Münster, Germany, important Protestant leaders in Ireland knew better.[26] And when political uncertainty did ensue in the winter of 1659–60 most Baptists did not add to the confusion. They did not support Lt-General Edmund Ludlow who had been sent over to Ireland by the military junta in London that was hostile to a full parliament sitting there and to the restoration of Charles II.[27]

After the king was restored Lawrence still had many friends who held significant rank and authority in Ireland. In 1662 the earls of Orrery, Mountrath and Anglesey vouched for him saying that he had been 'very Civile to ye King's friends' by preserving their estates that would have otherwise been destroyed' during the Interregnum. He also developed an amicable relationship with James Butler, now duke of Ormond and Lord Lieutenant of Ireland. Because Lawrence was interested in improving the economy of his

ing of Many Officers of the Army in England, at Windsor Castle, in the Year 1648 (London, 1659), title page; British Library, Lansdowne MS 822, f. 107.

24 *Thurloe State Papers*, v, p. 710.

25 R. Lawrence, *Gospel Seperation Seperated from its Uses* (London, 1657); *The Agreement and Resolution of the Ministers of Christ, Associated with the City of Dublin and the Province of Leinster* (Dublin, 1659).

26 Propagandists constantly reminded the public of disturbing events in sixteenth-century Germany. Two examples pertinent to Ireland are: George Pressick, *A brief Relation of some of the Most Remarkable Passages of the Anabaptists of High and Low Germany in the year 1521 &c.* ([Dublin], 1660); S. Ashton, *Satan in Samuel's Mantle, or the Cruelty of Germany acted in Jersey* (London, 1660).

27 British Library, Egerton MS 2542, f. 465; *An Account of the Chief Occurrences of Ireland (12 March–19 March)* (London, 1660); Edmund Ludlow, *A Voyce from the Watchtower*, A.B. Worden (ed), Camden Society, (1978), fourth series, pp. 251, 254,

newly adopted land Ormond solicited him to begin a woollen mill outside
Dublin at Chapelizod. Later, in 1669 when Lawrence ran into financial difficulties, resulting from the woollen mill, he attempted to gain compensation
from the government. The Irish Attorney General, Sir William Domville, and
Sir William Temple testified favourably on his behalf. Even though the ecclesiastical settlement imposed on Ireland after the Restoration made the Church
of Ireland a narrow body, the Protestant community was in reality no less
comprehensive than it was in the early seventeenth century.[28]

After all most Protestants had a common economic interest, holding on to
land acquired during Cromwellian rule and resisting the Catholic threat. The
upheaval of war and conquest during the 1640s and 1650s had led to a
massive confiscation of land owned by Roman Catholics in Ireland. Subsequently there were many land transfers, soldiers for example who received
their pay arrears in confiscated land, chose to sell rather than settle. There
was great uncertainty over titles to land giving a common economic and
political interest to Protestants of all varieties. The 'Protestant Interest' and
Catholic threat helped to paper over difficulties between Protestants of differing religious orientations. As the earl of Orrery commented, 'the more Protestants the merrier'.[29] Even though relations between nonconformists and
other Protestants varied from locality to locality Baptist settlers in late seventeenth-century Ireland did share in the political and economic expectations of
the greater Protestant community.

Due to Richard Lawrence's political influence he was the natural leader
and spokesman for the Irish Baptist community at this time. In November
1669 William Penn met Lawrence at a dinner in Dublin and complained in
his personal journal that Lawrence was 'Passionate & Confounded about
morall religion'.[30] It was true that his piety had changed since the heady days
of the 1640s. Liberality based on the hope of large-scale inward regeneration
of individuals was replaced with advocating measures that would insure that
individuals conform to outward moral standards. Whereas Lawrence had trusted
and favoured the preaching of the poor and lowly in the 1640s by 1668 his
opinion concerning the poor, at least in Ireland, was significantly altered. Due
to his experience at Chapelizod he recommended to the duke of Ormond that
overseers, inspecting the spinning work farmed out over the country, be made
commissioners of the peace. This was because the poor had a 'disposition to
disorder and Quarrels amongst themselves' in addition they had an 'Aptness

258; W.M. Brady (ed), *Clerical and Parochial Records of Cork, Cloyne and Ross* (3 vols.,
   Dublin, 1863–5), iii, p. 54.
28 Bodleian Library, Carte MSS 49, f. 643; 50, f. 38; 66, f. 303; 160, ff. 36–7.
29 T.C. Barnard, 'Tradition, Ethnicity and Identities in Protestant Dissent, 1650–1750'
   in Kevin Herlihy (ed) *The Irish Dissenting Tradition, 1650–1750* (Dublin, 1995), p. 31.
30 Richard Dunn and Mary Dunn (eds), *The Papers of William Penn* (2 vols., Philadel-
   phia, 1981), i, p. 120.

to defraud the Overseere and doe theire work deceitfully'. Despite his sullen view of the poor he did retain a somewhat affectionate regard for the godly ones and believed that it was the responsibility of those blessed with prosperity to help them lead productive lives. When Lawrence solicited Ormond to transfer the woollen mill at Chapelizod from government ownership to himself one of the main points of his argument was that the prayers of the poor were more efficacious and that those prayers would be an intercession for his personal welfare.[31]

This switch of emphasis is also borne out by Lawrence's publication of *The Interest of Ireland* in 1682. He was obsessed with outward moral conformity and the regulation of behaviour for the economic advancement of Irish society. He attacked all social and economic classes, but especially the upper classes because the lower ranks 'are more apt to imitate their Prince's vices than their virtues'. He wanted the affluent to be restricted by sumptuary laws because they engaged in 'wealth-consuming and trade obstructing debaucheries' in buying 'gay clothes, gaming, whoring and drunkenness'. For Lawrence there were two types of 'excessive consumption' with which the prosperous affianced, and therefore should be constrained by law. The first was 'the Belly' which concerned the importation of wine, fruit, spice and tobacco. The second was 'the Back' which involved the importation of 'Silk, fine Linnens, Silver and Gold-laces'. Lawrence believed that 'excessive consumption' by the wealthy, and not so wealthy, was draining the valuable resources of Ireland to foreign countries, especially Roman-Catholic France. Lawrence appealed to the authority of Martin Luther when he expressed the view that these imported commodities for 'the Back' served 'only for Pride, and no Profit'. Products associated with 'the Belly' such as wine led to other vices such as 'Whoring' which caused the parishes to be overburdened with 'bastards'.[32]

Rectitude, according to Lawrence, was an adamantine discipline akin to the regimentation of the military states of Sparta and Rome, who were 'no Fashion-mongers'. He commended the 'gravity of the Germans', whereas the powerful French were 'effeminate'. Ecomonic prodigality was bringing about a proliferation of vice and producing 'effeminate spirits'. Effeminacy was not so much associated with sex as with individuals simply becoming 'soft'. It is very understandable, due to Lawrence's military background, why his piety and perspective had changed to a conservative rule-oriented drive for societal reform. He was, however, not unusual, as the pious of all varieties were moving in this direction. For many years after the Glorious Revolution the impetus for social reform was couched in paradigms that emphasised training

31 Bodleian Library, Carte MS 35, f. 523.
32 Richard Lawrence, *The Interest of Ireland in its Trade and Wealth Stated* (London and Dublin, 1682), Part one, chapter one.

individuals to conform to outward moral precepts devised by the educated. In Ireland and England the short-lived Society for the Reformation for Manners epitomised this thought at the dawn of the eighteenth century. Many believed, with Lawrence, that economic prosperity was linked with adherence to moral maxims.[33]

III

Baptist piety, whether in England, Wales or Ireland ceased to be really unique after the Glorious Revolution, except in relation to the administration of baptism. In Ireland during the first half of the eighteenth century the Baptists had become rather conventional in their piety and perspective. Christianity was under assault on many fronts and the Baptists, especially in Ireland, were ill-equipped to confront the new intellectual challenges. Therefore, they looked to advocates from larger religious bodies, especially the Church of England, for guidance on larger issues of orthodoxy. Also, because many Irish Baptists had attained wealth and social respectability during the late seventeenth century they wanted to take part in the activities of the wider Protestant community. Unfortunately for them a significant division in the Protestant community appeared when the 'Protestant Interest' turned into the 'Protestant Ascendency' during the early years of the eighteenth century. In order to be a part of this elite portion of the Irish Protestant community one had to be wealthy and in communion with the Church of Ireland. Although a significant portion of Irish Baptist families were wealthy their religious aspirations precluded them from the higher reaches of this world of social respectability and esteem.

After the Williamite War Irish Baptists engaged in ecclesiastical reforms designed to promote closer affiliation among the several meetings in Ireland by establishing an Association and a scheme for training ministerial candidates. A great part of the motivation for having theologically trained ministers was to accommodate the sensibilities of the wider Protestant community. Although there were theologically trained men serving the community during the seventeenth century the greater portion of their leaders were untrained lay preachers who conducted conventicles in private homes. In the eighteenth century when they could be more open new meeting houses were built and preachers were sought who could present a pleasant appearance to the respectable in the outside world.[34] The changes that enabled more prominence

33 Ibid., chapter one; T.C. Barnard, 'Reforming Irish Manners: the religious societies in Dublin during the 1690s', in *Historical Journal*, xxxv (1992), pp. 805–38.
34 Baptist Union of Ireland, Belfast, Accompt of the Fund for the Education of young men for the Ministry [hereafter, The Trustees' Book], pp. 1–12; Baptist Church, Cork, Cork Baptist Church Book, pp. 22–4, 57, 76–7.

in the wider-world also proscribed individuals in their community from higher social rank and this became one of the most significant causes of Irish Baptist decline.

Irish Baptist constituents lacked social cohesion from their beginning because they were highly individualistic and many were evanescent members of the military establishment. The original members and those that followed, like many other Protestants in late seventeenth-century Ireland, came to Ireland without a specific religious motivation, but rather a specific economic one.[35] They came in the hope of improving themselves economically by land development, service or trade. Many of the families in the Irish Baptist community accomplished their economic aspirations which later led to defections by their progeny, especially male heirs. The exit of prominent families led to the subsequent loss of community esteem and the financial resources that were needed for establishing institutional stability.

The Cromwellian basis of the Irish Baptist community suffered further erosion after the Williamite War. No male heirs from Richard Lawrence's family remained in the Irish Baptist community, only a portion of female descendants remained faithful. Another prominent family with Cromwellian roots in Dublin was the Falkiner family. Michael Falkiner was the patriarch who joined with the Baptists soon after he came to Dublin in the late 1640s where he was engaged in the wool trade. He had three sons and three daughters; his eldest son died without issue, another named Sylvester was captured and sold into slavery on the Barbary coast, and his third son Daniel inherited. Daniel in turn also had three sons, the eldest and heir Daniel, along with John and Caleb. After inheriting the family fortune Daniel conformed to the established church which made it possible for him to become High Sheriff of Dublin in 1721 and later Lord Mayor of Dublin.[36] John Falkiner remained faithful to the Baptist community and had three daughters, all of whom married Dublin Baptists and were subscribing members of the congregation in Swift's Alley in the 1740s and 50s. Caleb Falkiner, the second son, removed to Cork, probably in the first decade of the eighteenth century, where he was a successful wool trader and banker.[37] He married Ruth Riggs, the

---

35 For an insightful analysis and description of late seventeenth-century Irish Protestants see T.C. Barnard, 'Crisis in the Protestant Identity, 1641–1685' in *Past and Present*, no. 127 (May, 1990).

36 B. Burke, *A Genealogical and Heraldic Dictionary of the Landed Gentry of Great Britain and Ireland* (London, 1858), pp. 365–6; Cork Baptist Church Book, pp. 14–7; Genealogical Office, Dublin, MS 103, p. 106; 'The Family of Falkiner; The Falkiners of Abbotstown' in *Journal of the Archaeological Society of County Kildare*, vii, no. 5 (1917), pp. 331–47.

37 Baptist Union of Ireland, Belfast, A Collection of Subsriptions for the Meeting at Swift's Alley, ff. 33–55; Cork Baptist Church Book, pp. 14–17; E. O'Kelly, *The Old Private Banks and Bankers of Munster* (Cork, 1959), p. 38.

daughter of a wealthy Cromwellian Baptist patron in Cork, 'about the year 1711', and had a son and daughter. His son, Riggs Falkiner, married a Baptist and became a deacon at the Cork Baptist meeting. Like his father he became a successful banker, but after his first wife's death in 1762 his interest in being a member of the Baptist community waned. In October 1764 he married Anne Marturin, who was the daughter of Gabriel Marturin, the dean of St Patrick's Cathedral in Dublin. Presumably he had conformed to the established church prior to the marriage. He then entered politics and became a member of the Irish Parliament until 1783 and died in April 1797. Just like his uncle Daniel's family all of his descendants remained in the established church.[38]

Another example of this widespread pattern of erosion was the Geale family in Kilkenny. John Geale and his wife Mary Earwalker came to Ireland in the late 1650s. John had been a cavalry soldier in the English parliamentary army, and when his regiment was disbanded he and Mary left England due to pressure from her relatives who believed that she had married below herself. On coming to Ireland they settled on a farm near Kilkenny town and immediately began advancing their family's economic prospects. When they retired they rented two houses in Kilkenny town and gave the use of one to the congregation. This was done at the instigation of Mary for she wanted to be nearer to 'the means of grace'. The couple had nine children, but only one continued in the Baptist faith. This was Joseph Geale. Part of the reason for his continuance was that his mother considered him 'her favorite' and that she held out the promise of her dowry if he kept up his spiritual commitments. When Joseph came of age, had married and 'kept a shop', Mary still withheld her fortune from him because she wanted to make sure that he 'retain'd his integrity'. When he left Kilkenny to take part in the Williamite War she gave him a 'pocket bible' and a Puritan devotional book written by the English Independent, John Flavel. On his return home she surreptitiously checked to see whether Joseph had made good use of her gifts by gaining access to his 'portmanteau' in asking for the key so that she could wash his linen. When she found 'what she desir'd wrapt up more carefully than anything there, yet not so nicely clean as not to discover that they had been made propper use of' she provided Joseph with the necessary capital for the purchase of a farm which vastly supplemented his annual income.[39]

Unfortunately for the Kilkenny Baptist meeting Joseph Geale would be their last benefactor. Joseph during his lifetime continued in the faith of his 'pious ancestors' and, like his parents, became the 'chief support of the Bap-

38 Cork Baptist Church Book, pp. 7, 14, 28, 47, 53, 62, 87; *Faulkner's Dublin Journal*, 9 January 1762, 16 October 1764; *Hibernian Chronicle*, 27 April 1797; O'Kelly, *The Old Private Banks*, pp. 38–9; *Biographical Dictionary of the Irish Parliament*, forthcoming.
39 *Memoirs Mistress Ann Fowkes* (Dublin, 1892), pp. 18–19.

tist Church in Kilkenny'. He provided the rent for a meeting house in the city, and sponsored family devotional exercises 'not on Sundays only' but 'for all the family, servants as well as children'. However, the motivation for his religious activity came primarily from his wife, Ann Lawrence, the daughter of Richard Lawrence, who herself had been froward concerning religion in her late adolescent years. But after 'God was pleas'd to exercise her with afflictions' she, according to her daughter, 'dived for precious pearls in sorrows stream, and there found them'. Just as the first generation of Irish Geales had been less than successful in keeping the children in the Baptist fold so it was with Joseph's family. The religious hopes of the Geale family rested on one male child and heir, Benjamin.[40]

The religious training that was a substantial part of the Geale family life did not have the desired effect on Benjamin. According to his sister Ann he had developed quite different tastes. He 'prefer'd the card-table to prayers' and later when he came into possession of the estate he removed 'the large Bible that us'd to lye in the parlour window' in order to make room for a 'dice-table'. His sister complained bitterly that her father had let her brother inherit the family fortune. According to Ann religion should have been the determining factor in deciding where the family fortune should have been placed. She believed that her father's behaviour toward Benjamin was 'partial' and that he was a 'favorite' to the 'disadvantage of the rest' of the children, even though 'no superior merit ever appeared in the favorite'. The row resulted in Ann being 'banished' by the behaviour of her father and brother toward her due to her protest. According to Ann her father had set up 'an idol in their family' which was 'that trifling ambition of keeping up a [family] name'. Her affront at her father's decision was expressed by saying that her father had spoke 'degradeingly of his daughters' because 'we were not like to keep up his name'. She argued from Scripture that the 'name of the just is blessed, but the name of the wicked shall rot'. She supplemented her argument with a text from St. Paul's letter to the Galatians that 'there is neither male or female, but all are one in Christ Jesus'.[41]

The defection of the affluent affected other communities as well. Such losses were not confined to the Irish Baptists. Even the Quakers, who were able to develop social and economic networks that gave incentive to the prosperous to stay within the fold, had their problems. A Quaker recorder in Cork exhibited dismay because a large estate 'went quite out of our Society' when the only surviving son of a Quaker family became prodigal. He laconically remarked, 'coming into his Fathers Inheritance Young & Foolish became a Prodigal, purchas' at the Heraldry Office the Title of Knight and Baronet,

40 Ibid., pp. 15–17.
41 Ibid., pp. 34–7

marry'd and soon after died'.[42] The economic resources of the wealthy had
been a major factor in the Irish Baptist community's ability to regenerate
itself in the early eighteenth century. Prosperous families had endowed an
education fund in Dublin to train those called to the ministry and also provided the means by which local meetings were able to hire trained pastors,
and build meeting houses. Socially mobile families not only hurt the community financially but—just as important—it also caused a loss of respect among
fellow Protestants.[43]

Although prominent personalities within the Irish Baptist community were
never a real part of the Protestant elite they did have a good standing in the
Protestant community at the turn of the eighteenth century. During the late
seventeenth century Richard Lawrence was a member of the Council of Trade
which advised the government on economic policy. He was also sheriff of
Dublin and was succeeded by another Baptist, Caleb Thomas, in that position. A protégé of Lawrence was Mordecai Abbot who was the orphaned son
of a Cromwellian soldier. Presumably through Lawrence's influence Abbot
was employed by the exchequer and after the Williamite War Abbot became
general receiver of revenue.[44] The Cork Baptist, Major Edward Riggs, was a
member of the Irish Parliament in the 1690s. He had a considerable estate in
County Cork and was able to send his son, also named Edward, to London to
study law. When he died in 1707 he naturally left the bulk of his estate to
Edward, but set aside a portion of his estate for the use his widow Ann which
amounted to an income of £500 per annum.[45] His other son, Thomas, became
involved with a Huguenot sect called the New Prophets (or French Prophets)
which led to his arrest and conviction at Drogheda in 1712. Because the
magistrate knew and respected his father, Thomas was let off with a fine
rather than whipping, branding or imprisonment.[46] In Kilkenny Joseph Geale's
place in society enabled him to resist affronts to Baptists there. When trouble
came because the civil authorities wanted to break up the meeting he 'aw'd
the justice and parson' by 'talking roundly to them'. Joseph also enjoyed
popularity in the local community through his talents as a barber-surgeon.
His ability to use the lance 'both in bleeding and opening of wounds ...
rendered himself usefull to his tennants and poor neighbours'.[47] The early

42 Society of Friends Historical Library, Dublin, Cork Marriage Register, f. 1.
43 The Trustee's Book, p. 2; Cork Baptist Church Book, pp. 3–24; *The Memoirs of Ann
    Fowkes*, pp. 20–1.
44 Trinity College Library, Dublin, MS 847, ff. 1–7; *Memoirs of Ann Fowkes*, p. 32;
    Nicholls, *Original Letters and Papers*, p. 149; *Calendar of the Treasury Rolls*, part iii, p.
    1319, part v, p. 1924.
45 *Biographical Dictionary of the Irish Parliament*; Cork Baptist Church Book, pp. 14–17.
46 *The Tryal and Conviction of Thomas Riggs and John Woods Pretended Prophets, Who
    were Try'd at Drogheda, April 13, 1712* (Dublin, 1712), pp. 11–12.
47 *Memoirs of Ann Fowkes*, pp. 20–1.

eighteenth-century Irish Baptists, for the most part, enjoyed a fair amount of social regard due to having a significant number of members who were deemed respectable by not only their Protestant neighbours but society at large.

The Irish Baptists, like other dissenters, placed a great deal of emphasis on education. Due to their belief in not 'imposing the name of Christian on those whose age rendered them incapable of choice' they thought it extremely important to give their children the necessary tools to make the right religious decision. Education and religious training was considered to be one and the same thing by most segments of society. In 1725 the pastor of the Cork Baptist meeting complained that Baptist parents were allowing their children to marry 'the children of men' who had a 'differing education'. In the late 1740s two converts to the Baptists were said to have been 'educated in the Church of England'. Later in 1760, a Roman Catholic convert, Miles Crowly, claimed 'that we should not reject our old Principles in which we have been educated, till we have carefully examined them'.[48] The primary purpose of educating Baptist children was to instruct them in a piety which led to salvation. This piety was to be 'directed from knowledge' and 'from the information of a well instructed mind'. Piety was a discipline that the children learned through the pastor's preaching at meeting, family discussion of the sermon, family prayer, personal prayer and reading the Bible and devotional works. Children were encouraged to seek a salvation experience through conviction of sin. They were to 'count the cost of religion' so that they might not later 'fall off in a day of trial and become a scandal to it'. Personal prayer or private devotions were to be learned so that the discipline 'soon became not only familiar, but sometimes delightfull'. When a child reached adolescence and wanted to become a full-fledged member of the meeting there had to be examination by the minister, followed by an appearance before the congregation to give a testimony of faith and be questioned concerning the applicants experience of faith. In 1704 at Kilkenny a member of the congregation asked, Ann Geale, a twelve year old postulant if she could truly say that she 'lov'd Jesus Christ above all things'. This was asked because this type of personal encounter 'surpass'd all other experience'. Therefore, those joining were expected to adopt a spiritual posture of resignation which placed all earthly concerns secondary. The high moral standard of behaviour expected of the

48 Angus Library, Regents Park, Oxford, Backus MS, History of the Warren Association, appendix, p. 6; Cork Baptist Church Book, pp. 31, 41; Kevin Herlihy, 'The early Eighteenth-Century Irish Baptists: Two Letters' in *Irish Economic and Social History*, xix (1992), pp. 71–5; Miles Crowly, *A Narrative of the Case of Miles Crowly, containing, His Reasons for quitting the Communion of the Church of Rome, and embracing the Protestant Religion* (Dublin, 1760), p. 8. Also printed below in this volume, pp. 112–20. For the relationship between education and religion see David D. Hall, *Worlds of Wonder, Days of Judgement* (Cambridge, 1990), chapter one.

initiated produced a perception of the world that was fraught with constant anxiety and tension. One was to have 'zeal with candor and moderation'; they were to possess 'sobriety and seriousness with cheerfulness'; they were to have 'cheerfulness without anything inclining to sallies of levity', and exercise 'just authority without severity'. Ideally those claiming an experience of faith were to repudiate the world and live primarily for the next. Due to the harsh personal discipline the temptation of 'unbelief and despondency' led some to speculate that since they could not 'expect to enjoy the pleasures of another world 'twere better to indulge as much' as one can in this one. While others, as a Baptist pastor exhorted at a funeral in 1771, chose 'to be patient and resigned' and to 'live in actual readiness for your great change and be follow-ers of them who thro' faith and patience are now inheriting the promises'. As we have seen many of the affluent chose the former option.[49]

By the middle of the eighteenth century attrition had taken its toll on the Irish Baptist community. In the early part of that century Catholic political power had been reduced considerably due to the downfall of James II, but as the century progressed Catholic resurgence sometimes expressed itself in ag-gression. Members of the Church of Ireland who held political power were sometimes able manipulate and direct that aggression as in the case of rioting against the Methodists at Cork city in 1749. Likewise the Baptists, because of their loss of social prestige, became vulnerable to popular aggression in the second half of the eighteenth century. When the Irish Baptist Association called for a day of fast in 1775 for the 'revival of religion and with a view to the distressed state of our brethren in America' the Cork Baptist meeting refused. They claimed that the Irish government considered the Americans traitors and 'the Papists', who had recently worked out a formula for taking an oath of allegiance, 'would be glad of an opportunity to demonstrate their zeal by disturbing our meeting the same week'.[50]

In addition many in the Church of Ireland expressed social contempt toward the Baptists which could lead to ugly incidents. In 1752 the assistant to the Cork pastor, Morgan Edwards, claimed 'when Christianity is intro-duced with power into a family or neighbourhood it will certainly cause some disturbances and it is the same with regard to individuals for Christianity causes great disturbances and trouble of mind'. Around this time there had been a fair number of civil disturbances in Cork as a result of religious tension. In May 1749 the mayor of Cork, a member of the Church of Ireland, allowed a mob led by a peculiar ballad singer, Nicholas Butler, to harass the Methodist meeting by causing a ten-day riot. The foment resulted in assaults

49 *Memoirs of Ann Fowkes*, pp. 42–5; Colgate-Rochester Theological Seminary, Rochester, New York, Sermons of Morgan Edwards, unpaginated and unfoliated, James 3:17, 17 September 1752; Cork Baptist Church Book, pp. 7–11, 91–3.
50 Cork Baptist Church Book, p. 112.

and throwing debris from the street on those belonging to the meeting. About the same time disruption occurred during a funeral at the Baptist burial ground in Cork, attended by a mixture of Baptists and Methodists, when stones were thrown over the wall.[51]

On a more personal level changes in religious conviction could lead to particularly nasty interactions between supposed loved ones. In the 1740s Jane Abbot, daughter of a wealthy Church of Ireland merchant in Cork, married John Trayer, an unbaptised Baptist, and dolor soon followed. Due to a casual discussion about baptism between her husband and a clergyman Jane began making her own inquiry into the validity of infant baptism. She later spoke to her husband about her 'doubts' concerning infant baptism, but he 'rather strove to stifle them and discourage any further inquiry'. John did not want to alienate his father-in-law because of 'the loss he might sustain'. Even so Jane continued her personal investigation and began to attend the Baptist meeting 'more frequently'. Despite not mentioning her new convictions her mother noticed her absence from the established church services. The mother interrogated her daughter and discovered her defection. As a result 'she struck her daughter severely'. As this was taking place her father, 'who always had a great authority over her', returned home and 'joined his wife in such threatening and terrifying language as gave a shock to Mrs. Trayer and was supposed to occasion her miscarriage'. The torrent eventually involved the bishop of Clogher, Dr Robert Clayton, who was unable to dissuade her. Disturbance increased as Jane was physically assaulted in the streets, along with other members of the Baptist meeting. Harassment came to an end on 18 December 1754 when Jane 'was released from this scene of persecution and called to the silent grave'.[52]

Another instance shows that Trayer's case was not isolated. After Mrs Wilson was baptised on 28 July 1749 she returned home to find that her husband 'who was a zealous Methodist' was enraged and forced her out of the house. In order to be allowed back home she had to promise that she would not 'join in communion' with the Baptists. She even had to suffer the ignimony of her daughter, who was also 'a zealot', scandalising her as an 'Anabaptist, a turncoat' at the Methodist meeting.[53]

---

51 Sermons of Morgan Edwards, James 3:17, 16 August 1752; David Hempton, *Methodism and Politics in British Society 1750–1850* (London, 1984), p. 35; Cork Baptist Church Book, p. 40.

52 Shortly after this incident Clayton himself was charged with heresy, but died before the matter was adjudicated. The controversy led to a discussion between Sir John Percival, Lord Egmont, the bishop of Oxford and Clayton about the relationship of Baptists and the established church. *Manuscripts of the Earl of Egmont, Diary of the First Earl of Egmont* (3 vols., London, 1923) iii, pp. 316–17; Cork Baptist Church Book, pp. 31–5.

53 Cork Baptist Church Book, pp. 40–1.

The few affluent members who chose to abide in their familial faith were extolled by other Baptists, and this praise reveals much about their temperment and outlook. The Cork banker Caleb Falkiner, when he died in 1746, was remembered because 'he continued steadfast notwithstanding the increase in his fortune and the inducements he had to seek after the honours and titles of the world'. When another wealthy Cork banker, Stephen Mills, died unexpectedly in 1770 he was venerated because 'admist the temptations of a gay and flattering world to which his fortune and rank in life exposed him he continued steadfast in his holy profession'.[54] Clearly, the Irish Baptists saw wealth and worldly success as detrimental to their faith. Ann Fowkes's children had 'heaped up riches in abundance' by trading in Portugal which she considered 'a barren and wicked country'. They had done it 'with a clear conscience', but her son Larry's disposition had 'sadly alter'd'. He had 'an air of gaiety', bordering on 'levity', and on the Lord's day went to the parks and gardens. Even though he did 'acknowledge the vanity and emptiness of all earthly enjoyments' he pursued such enjoyment 'as if there was no other happiness'.[55] In January 1751 the Cork congregation was warned about 'the immoderate cares of this world' because 'they pine the seed of the Word in their heart and choke it' and 'they make the soul meager and barren'.[56] The possibilities for amusement, enjoyment, or even indulgence, that wealth created was ideally to be shunned. However, prosperity, created by industry and self-denial, presented fascination and allurement for their offspring, especially the male ones interested in ambitious social and economic pursuits.

I V

The Baptist leaders began with a theology of confident expectation. In the 1640s they anticipated that a great change would be wrought by God in the world, and they believed that they had a major role in shaping the transformation. Soon after such dreams dissipated their attention and effort took a new direction. In the late seventeenth century Lawrence, even though he had modified his vision, was still interested in using his skill and influence for societal improvement. However, the most prominent feature of his thought had altered from an anticipation of God changing the hearts of men through liberality to a reliance on discovering moral design. Baptists, whether in England, Wales or Ireland, were forced during the late seventeenth century to abandon efforts to reach those outside their community and to concentrate

54 Ibid., pp. 14, 89.
55 *Memoirs of Ann Fowkes*, pp. 182–5.
56 Sermons of Morgan Edwards, Matthew 13:3–8, 7 January 1751.

instead on inculcating their own children. As the Irish Baptists placed stress on refining moral virtue to an unreachable standard they created an unattractive situation for their progeny. Their piety and perspective was not all that different from other dissenters in Ireland, or anywhere else in the English-speaking world, but theirs was a fragile community. The 'decay of religion' was widespread in the early eighteenth century, but many religious societies, especially those outside of Ireland, were able to rebound through religious revivals and other evangelisation efforts in mid-century. The hapless Irish Baptists though were not able to recover from their far-reaching losses. Commercial growth, austerity and class-consciousness had conspired against them. By the late eighteenth century their piety and perception was so introspective that they were easily dismissed, marginalised and ill-defined by those outside their community.

Spiritual Perception and the Evolution of the Irish Quakers

RICHARD S. HARRISON

Although there has been a good amount of historical revision about the spiritual origins of the Society of Friends it is generally accepted that it grew out of the Puritan movement.[1] Quakers themselves saw their religion, in William Penn's words, as 'primitive christianity revived'.[2] They saw their rediscovery as a spatial metaphor of 'inwardness' contrasted with the 'outwardness' of more formal contemporary religion.[3] According to the early Quakers there had been a 'long night of apostasy' which was a decline from the Christianity of the first believers.[4] The attempt of the Protestants to break from apostasy had merely perpetuated many of the errors of popery in new forms and ceremonies. These early Quakers wanted to finally lay an axe to the root of a corrupt tree because Christ had come to teach the people himself.[5] Therefore, the Quakers bore testimony to the peaceable gospel of Jesus, but knew that they themselves had been called to the 'War of the Lamb'—a war with spiritual weapons and social consequences.[6] Their views were not a mere

1 Kenneth L. Carroll, 'Quakerism and the Cromwellian Army in Ireland' in *Journal of the Friends Historical Society* [hereafter *JFHS*], 54, no. 3 (1978), pp. 135–54. See also T.C. Barnard, *Cromwellian Ireland* (Oxford, 1975), pp. 109–12. For questions of historical revision see Thomas D. Hamm, 'George Fox and the Politics of Late Nineteenth Century Quaker Historiography' in Michael Mullett (ed) *New Light on George Fox, 1624–91* (York, 1993); and Melvin Bendy, 'The Interpretation of Quakerism, Rufus Jones and his Critics in *Quaker History* (1981) dxx, no. 1, pp. 3–21.

2 William Penn, 'Primitive Christianity' in *William Penn; The Peace of Europe and other writings with an Introduction by Joseph Besse* (Everyman Edition, London, nd), pp. 231–76.

3 Maurice A Creasey, *Inward and Outward: a Study in early Quaker language* (London, 1962).

4 Thomas Wight and John Rutty, *A History of the Rise and Progress of the People called Quakers in Ireland* (Dublin, 1751), pp. 5–78; 'The Preface (1714)' by John Stoddart in William Edmundson, *Journal of the Life and Travels of William Edmundson* (3rd edition, Dublin, 1820), pp. v–ix.

5 Robert Barclay's work was first printed in Latin in 1676. Numerous other editions followed in many of the major languages of Europe. A handy and usually available edition is, Robert Barclay, An *Apology for the True Chistian Divinity* (Glasgow, 1886), pp. 193–245, and especially p. 198.

6 Lewis Benson, *Catholic Quakerism* (Gloucester, 1966), pp. 41–5; James Naylor, *The*

form of Bible-centred Protestant individualism, but had an important communal significance. Their outlook was based on an absolute declaration of the 'priesthood of all believers' which was expressed through their meetings for worship.

I

Quaker theology was linked to concepts of light. The metaphor of light was frequently employed in their writings. They took a special interest in the Gospel of John where the metaphor of light is recurrent.[7] This light was no natural light but one that showed them their own darkness and led them to God. This was the light of Christ within, the light of conscience and of the Holy Spirit which alone could illuminate the scriptures. According to Friends this light led to unity and to a form of church organisation which duplicated the church of believers from long ago. For contemporaries this doctrine of light was the chief difficulty for understanding them. This measure of belief also made them independent of any human hierarchy and provided a disturbing challenge to other man-made traditions. Despite this, Quaker belief was not merely reactive because, for Quakers, their 'negations' really constituted affirmations.

Central to their point of view was the ideal of a free and unpaid ministry which was one of the major reasons why their resistance to tithes for the support of any established church was crucial to them. Numerous unpaid Quaker preachers, young and old, men and women, set off on long missionary journeys to transmit the gospel message they felt themselves called to deliver. They saw before them a world-wide mission following nothing but an internal imperative in which their brethren acquiesced. Their many journeys between Ireland, England, America and other places made the Friends an international order.[8] As early as 1663 at least four Friends who had been ministering in Ireland visited America. John Perrot and John Love, both of whom had also spent time in Ireland, went to call upon the Pope himself and suffered unspeakable tortures for their effort.[9]

Lamb's War (1658), reprinted in Hugh Barbour and Arthur Roberts (eds), *Early Quaker Writings* (Michigan, 1973), pp. 102–16.

7 Gospel of John, 1:4–5, 8:12 are some examples.

8 Frederick Tolles, *Quakers and the Atlantic Culture* (New York, 1960) passim; idem, *The Atlantic Community of the early Friends* (London, 1952).

9 Kenneth Carroll, *John Perrot, early Quaker schismatic* (London, 1971) See also list of early Quaker ministers in appendix to Tolles, *Atlantic Community* and William Sewell, *The History of the Rise and Progress ... of the Quakers* (2nd ed, corrected, London, 1725), p. 249 and other entries.

The Society of Friends provided a home for those who were torn between conflicting spiritual ideologies. It has been suggested that the Quaker rationale emerged from a Puritan milieu. However, the movement first appeared in northern English districts where there was no real Puritan tradition like that found in south-east England.[10] In many places it took over a population schooled by the Baptists. It was welcomed among the Celtic peoples in Cornwall and Wales, but not in Scotland.[11] The stress that Quakers put on consensus proved satisfying to their spiritual needs because it provided a suitable medium for the resolution of political, religious, cultural and intellectual differences on the island of Britain.

In Ireland the situation was unique. Quaker viewpoints were congenial to many in the Cromwellian army who found Independent and Baptist teaching wanting. Their spirituality offered a new awareness or realisation that was attractive to many. Another advantage was that the Quakers had a core of members that originated in north-west England giving them a relative degree of homogeneity.[12] Even though they were wearied of the time serving ideology of a Protestant state church and the lonely individualism of dissent they had no wish to identify themselves with the traditional religion of the native population. Democratic discussion and consensus politics experienced by soldiers in the Cromwellian army also contributed to initial Irish Quaker growth. In turn army discipline, which was spiritualised, helped to strengthen the Irish Friends.

Early Quaker theology was not particularly sympathetic to Ireland's Roman Catholic population. When Quaker ideas were first introduced in 1654 their preachers confined their message to the garrisons and English-speaking people. Paradoxically, in spite of having a world-wide message very little effort was put into evangelising the Irish-speaking people. But there were a few Irish converts such as Marcus Lynch of Galway, and Katherine McLoughlin who preached in Irish at Lurgan.[13] The Quaker patriarch George Fox even appealed to the Irish language in one of his thirty-one examples to demonstrate the the the Quaker doctrine of the universality of 'plain language'.[14]

---

10 Christopher Hill, *The World Turned Upside Down* (London, 1975), pp. 73–81. Also, Barry Reay, The Quakers and the English Revolution (London, 1985), pp. 27–31.
11 Information on the origins of Welsh Quakers is found in Philip Jenkins, *A History of Modern Wales, 1536–1990* (London, 1992), pp. 136–7; and G.F. Nuttall, *The Welsh Saints, 1640–1660* (Cardiff, 1957). A note on Friends in Scotland will be found in John Punshon, *Portrait in Gray; A Short History of the Quakers* (London, 1984), p. 69. Cornish Quakers need much more historical research, but see, George Fox's *Journal*; and *Records of the Sufferings of Friends in Cornwall, 1655–86* (London, 1928).
12 Isabel Grubb, 'Conditions in Ireland in the 17th and 18th Centuries as illustrated by Early Quaker Records', M.A. thesis, University of London, 1916, appendix.
13 Kenneth L. Carroll, 'Quakerism in Connaught, 1656–1978' in *JFHS*, div, 4 (1979), especially pp. 185, 189, 191; and Wight and Rutty, *History*, pp. 141–2.
14 George Fox and Benjamin Furly, *The Battledoor for Singular and Plural*.

In 1669 administrative meetings were established in Ireland which reflected the spiritual experience of Friends.[15] These meetings resonated the emotional and spiritual maturity achieved by the Society. Although based on consensus it was clear that the meeting was the preserve of a committed and inspired leadership in which the wider group acquiesced. The conflict between those who pleaded for excess of liberty for the individual and those who hungered for more external control was resolved by these meetings. Irish Friends, aware of unhappy separations in England, were able to use discipline effectively, thereby avoiding schism.[16]

Another important function of the administrative meetings was in handling relations with governmental authority and the wider community. These meetings supervised marriage and apprenticeship procedures, education, as well as the registration of births and deaths. In addition, the meetings encouraged a high standard of moral and ethical behaviour along with group discipline which was a crucial factor in communal survival and even, though not originally intended, commercial success.[17] Spiritual enthusiasm to a large extent was also brought under control. A typical example is John Exham of Charleville. Many believed that his method of witness was too extravagant and tended to undermine rather than help Friends. A delegation from the meeting was sent to discuss the matter with him.[18] Another Charleville Friend, Abigail Boles, was prominent and valued in the ministry, began to 'walk disorderly' and eventually permitted herself to be married by a 'priest'. Later, a little before her death, she was reconciled.[19]

II

For a religious movement that emphasised the activity of the divine in the here and now, in both individual and communal spirituality, the Quakers were obsessed with record keeping and leaving testimonies of their own history. Quakers were self-conscious of their mission which they saw in Judaic and Biblical terms. Their writing had an eye to the future. George Fox certainly designed his own spiritual journal for publication.[20] In 1700 when the Friends

15 Edmundson, *Journal*, p. 83.
16 Joseph Pike, *Some Account of the Life of* ... (London, 1837), pp. 41–2.
17 Richard S. Harrison, Dublin Quakers in Business, 1800–50, M.Litt. thesis, Trinity College, Dublin, i, pp. 12–20; Phil Kilroy, *Protestant Dissent and Controversy in Ireland, 1660–1714* (Cork, 1994), pp. 90–4.
18 Richard S. Harrison, 'The Quakers in Charleville' in *Journal of the Cork Historical and Archaeological Society* (1990), xcv, p. 57.
19 Ibid., p. 57.
20 Larry Ingle, 'George Fox, Historian' in *Quaker History* (1993), dxxxii, pp. 28–35.

decided to produce a history of themselves in Ireland it was a factor contributing to, or at least representing, group cohesion and identity.[21] The decision also reflected an awareness that the older leaders were dying out. Another feature tending to social cohesion was the distribution and reading of epistles sent out by the London Yearly Meeting and the Dublin Half-Yearly Meeting. These letters were read in local meetings and contained spiritual encouragement along with admonitions on undesirable behaviour. In addition testimonies and pious obituaries helped to forge positive patterns of religious behaviour. The Friends also subsidised books such as the Scots Quaker Robert Barclay's *Apology for the True Christian Divinity*.[22]

Barclay had been reared in a Calvinist home, but had also received a Jesuit education in France. His *Apology*, originally written in Latin, was designed to present Quaker doctrine in a theological and scholastic frame. Because Friends believed that the Bible itself was secondary to its own inspiration Barclay's work was important in showing the consonance of Friends views with the Bible. His work was specifically aimed at the Calvinist doctrine of predestination while affirming the perfectionist doctrine that sin can be overcome by individuals in this world. The *Apology* continued to play an important part in developing the Quaker frame of mind over the next three hundred years by sustaining a religion based on individual inward illumination in the context of meeting for worship. According to Barclay the effect on the individual in the silent meeting would be to 'feel the evil weakening and the good raised up'.[23] Unlike traditional Protestants these meetings were not to be grounded on words, or even silence, but in 'a holy dependence of the mind on God'. Worship lasted for hours with men and women seated on either side of the meeting house and the elders and 'recorded' ministers seated in the gallery at the head.

Emerging from this group identity came a special Quaker meaning for the word 'truth'. It did not refer to some abstract ideology, but rather to a living inward spiritual perception which was expressed 'outwardly' in plain dress and language, testimonies and simplicity. These outward signs gave group definition through an implicit exclusion of those who did not conform. Also, these signs were a tool for survival because their uniformity created positive expectations in the wider community. Although they were closely identified with the wider Irish Protestant community this radical spirituality was sometimes perceived as subversive. Ignorance led many to believe that Quakers were really Catholics or even Jesuits in disguise.[24] Therefore, a calculated withdrawal was part of the price for survival. As a result Friends gradually

21 Wight and Rutty, *History*, p. 81; Kilroy, *Protestant Dissent*, p. 99.
22 Robert Barclay, *Apology for the True Christian Divinity* (Glasgow, 1886).
23 Ibid., p. 255.
24 For example, Kilroy, *Protestant Dissent*, pp. 142, 153, 203–5.

achieved accommodation when the state allowed them to affirm rather than swear to an oath.[25] However, as late as 1722, a false charge alleging treason with Jacobites was given credence.[26]

Verbal ministry in worship was open to everyone present as long as they were responding to the leading of the Holy Spirit. As the Quaker movement became more established communal recognition was given to those who had a more frequent and powerful calling. Recognition came after long prayerful consideration and was recorded in books. If a 'recorded minister' developed powerful 'concerns' which led to the desire to serve at another meeting first the administrative meeting of the Men or Women had to 'unite in the concern'. After prayerful consideration the administrative meeting would issue a certificate which was to be presented and endorsed by each group visited by the minister.

Although Friends were bound together by a multitude of commercial and family links these ministers played an important role in uniting Irish Friends with those in Britain and America into one great spiritual family.[27] In the early eighteenth century there were numerous ministerial visitors to Ireland; between 1699 and 1720 there were at least 355.[28] Afterwards there was a decline, but never a discontinuance. These ministering men and women had great spiritual sensitivity allowing them to tend to the needs of individuals and groups which was known in the community as 'speaking to their condition'.

These ministering Friends claimed that there was an 'openness to truth' in Ireland, primarily among the Protestant population.[29] In 1710 John Fallowfield, a 'public' or ministering Friend, travelled to visit small groups of Friends as far west as Baltimore, Skibbereen and Castlesalem. In Bantry many people attended his ministry and were 'generally well-affected', except for 'some Papists'. In Kinsale there was a recently built meeting house and Fallowfield claimed the English were 'generally well-satisfied', but 'the Irish Papists were troublesome, partly for want of room and partly their wonted behaviour when they heard the testimony of Truth against their superstitions and idolatry'.[30] Animosity was not always the case however. There was a satisfactory spiritual discussion between a Roman Catholic and Thomas Story, a visiting ministering Friend, who reported, 'we parted in friendship, with good wishes on either side'.[31]

25 Wight and Rutty, *History*, pp. 283, 292.
26 George Bewley, *Narrative of the Christian Experiences of George Bewley, late of the City of Cork, Deceased* (Dublin, 1750), pp. 29–31.
27 See above, note 8.
28 Bewley, *Narrative*, p. 39.
29 Wight and Rutty, *History*.
30 'Record of Friends Travelling in Ireland, 1654–1765' in *JFHS* (1913), x, 3, pp. 157–80.
31 Wight and Rutty, *History*, pp. 255–62.

In Ulster an English Friend Benjamin Holme was on one of several visits to Ireland in 1712 when he held a large meeting that was attended by Presbyterians. As a result, on the request of Ulster Friends, the Half-Yearly Meeting published Holme's, *Concerning the Universal Love of God to Mankind and against that erroneous principle of absolute predestination to all Eternity*. The following year 2,000 copies of Barclay's *On Predestination* were printed for distribution to the Calvinist Presbyterians. Later, in 1724, Holme noted that the Presbyterians were divided because those adhering to 'New Light' theology refused to subscribe to the Westminster Confession.[32]

A number of determined Irish-based Friends conducted frequent visitations to Connacht. One of these was George Rooke who often accompanied visiting ministers to remote districts. Rooke himself was probably, like his wife, an Irish-speaker which perhaps helped his ministry because native Irish Catholics did come into the Quaker fold.[33] In Cootehill, County Cavan, Terence Cayle and his wife are described in Quaker records as being 'native Irish'.[34] Other instances are the Malones of Carlow, the Tomeys of Cork, the Doyles of Wexford and the Carrolls of Ulster and later Cork.[35] These families constituted Quaker dynasties. It is also worth noting that these native Irish who joined the Quakers were not the result of assimilation mediated by the wider Protestant community.

In spite of their claims to a world-wide mission difficulties emerged for Friends. Given that personal access to the Divine was a possibility for every human-being there seemed little urgency in seeking sectarian converts. Even where their message was of interest to the wider population there was only a slight inclination to actually join the Friends. This conflicting attitude is apparent in Irish Friends' behaviour toward the wider community. As the eighteenth century progressed they became less anxious to initiate controversy and only responded in print to views which they believed maligned their ideas.[36]

Although Friends tried to demarcate themselves spiritually they were not

---

32 Ibid., p. 229. See also, Benjamin Holme, *A Collection of the Epistles and Works of ...* (London, 1754), p. 43.

33 For a biographical account of George Rooke, see Mary Leadbeater, *Biographical Notices* (London, 1823), pp. 129, 212–26.

34 John Fothergill, *An Account of the Life and Travels in the Work of the Ministry* (London, 1753), p. 210.

35 Richard S. Harrison, 'The Carroll Family of Cork: A Quaker Business Dynasty' in *JFHS* (1994), dvii, i, pp. 33–51. Information about other native Irish Quakers derive from abstracts of births, marriages, deaths and miscellaneous genealogical information in the Society of Friends Historical Library, Dublin (hereafter DFHL).

36 An example of formal debate is found in *An Exact Narrative of the Most Material Passages in a Late Dispute in Skinner's Alley between Oswald Edwards, Baptist, John Stoddart, Quaker, and Josiah Gill his Assistant* (Dublin, 1722).

always successful. At Dublin there was a woman who had married a Friend and ceased attending meeting after she was widowed. When she was questioned she stated that Protestants were all much alike, so it seemed not to matter where she worshipped.[37] An Englishwomen, Elizabeth Ashbridge, lived in Dublin and learned to speak Irish. She discussed religion with a good friend of hers who was Roman Catholic and even considered converting. However, her religious doubts were resolved when a priest told her that her co-religionists were damned and she would be damned unless she believed that James, son of the Pretender, was the legitimate king of England. She was thereby confirmed in her Quaker beliefs and went on to become a Quaker minister.[38]

We have seen that the Irish Quaker community was marked out by testimony and peculiarity, but wealth and their endogamous marriage practice also contributed to their survival as a distinct community. This same wealth also constituted one of the biggest threats to the spirituality of their community. Spiritually aware Quakers continually warned about wealth which was a frequent theme in the disciplinary meetings and epistles. A visiting preacher, Samuel Bownas, found the Irish Friends hard and indifferent. A contemporary explained to him that whilst they were very strict the 'leaven of the pharisees' was too much in evidence in their concern about outward things.[39]

As the more inspired leadership passed away caution and control seemed to become the emphasis of the Men's and Women's Meetings. There was a failure to bring the wider constituency into the decision making process. The consensus established did not encourage initiative or innovation in religious matters and assumed that inherited structures and practices were sacrosanct. Friends had departed from the experimental approach to spirituality of the first generation. Their doctrine which now facilitated caution, in turn allowed for accommodation with the state and for communal survival as well.

Caution extended to literature which can be seen in sporadic attempts to provide instructive models through their own literature. In 1733 Samuel Fuller produced a *Catechism* in an effort to promote religious instruction for children. Primarily it was based on Barclay's *Apology*.[40] The point of instruction was not to encourage a questioning mind, at least as far a religion was concerned. Epistles, both Irish and English, were chiefly concerned with admonishing their people to avoid atheistic books and spiritual infidelity. The

37 Dublin Monthly Meeting Minutes, vi, mo, 1758 (DFHL) MM, II, A.12 (1758–67).
38 'Account of the Life of Elizabeth Ashbridge' in *American Friends Library* (np, 1840), iv.
39 'Life of Samuel Bownas' in *American Friends Library*, iii, p. 41.
40 Samuel Fuller, *Some Principles and Precepts of the Christian Religion, A Catechism* (Dublin, 1733). Another edition was order in 1744 to be circulated. 420 were to go to Ulster, 680 to Leinster and 200 to Munster.

guidance indicates that there was a high literacy rate in the Quaker community that had to be controlled. A London Yearly Meeting epistle also warned against 'vile and corrupt books' which 'manifestly tend to oppose and reject the divine authority of the Holy Scriptures and to introduce deism, atheism and all manner of infidelity'.[41] Elizabeth Carleton, who grew up in the 1730s and 40s, illustrates Quaker caution in this area. She had an artistic inclination with a musical ear and fine voice. In addition she excelled at needlework and had a great interest in books. However she found many books which purported to 'promote virtue' and 'render vice odious' actually encouraged a disregard of Scripture.[42]

Despite their caution there was still a widespread interest in Quaker teachings. When Benjamin Holme came on his sixth visit in 1735 he travelled to Lixnaw in County Kerry and further on to Tralee and Dingle. Friends were not well-known there, even so, the Protestant gentlemen of the county displayed respect and friendship. On a visit to Millstreet the mention of the word 'purgatory' led to a number of hearers saying in Irish 'come away'.[43] In 1738 the visit of May Drummond, a Scotswoman, caused excitement in Cork. The novelty lay not only in her being a woman from Edinburgh, but on account of her aristocratic origins and her recent conversion to the Quakers. Another point of attraction may have been her supposed masculine appearance and speech. When a cleric, probably from the Church of Ireland, attempted to dissuade his congregation from attending her sermons, her visit encouraged adverse newspaper attention. Excerpts of her sermons were published so that the readers could make up their own minds. Her messages set out Quaker beliefs and were fairly innocuous and inoffensive to any particular sectarian perspective.[44]

Even though there was an openness to their ideas Irish Friends themselves were concerned about the low state of their own community. When David Hall, an English Friend, visited in 1737 he wrote an epistle which the National Meeting printed for wider circulation.[45] The letter encouraged better attendance at meetings, living within one's means, maintaining the plain language and avoiding marriages before priests (which was the prime cause of disownment at that time). The most notable feature of the admonishment was its concentration on behaviour rather than doctrine. Hall's visit also assisted

---

41 Rufus M. Jones, The Later Periods of Quakerism (2 vols. , London, 1921), i, p. 6n.
42 Elizabeth Shackleton, *Memoirs and Letters of* ... (London, 1822).
43 Wight and Rutty, *History*, pp. 321–32.
44 *The Serio-Jocular Medley* (Cork, 1738).
45 Wight and Rutty, *History*, p. 323 notes the chief heads of David Hall's *Epistle* of 1737. The National Meeting for Ireland ordered the printing of 1,500 copies to be 'on good paper and character and stitched with blue paper', Half-Yearly Meeting Minutes, iii mo, 1738 (DFHL), ½ YM A.3 (1708–57).

in the formalisation of a series of queries on the living practices of Friends, both socially and spiritually. A similar operation had been recently inaugurated by the London Yearly Meeting in 1740 the National Half-Yearly Yearly Meeting codified these queries and later thought it best that each Monthly Meeting submit written answers.[46] There were twenty-one queries and they were dealt with in batches, a few at a time, by the Monthly and Provincial Meetings. The answers were prayerfully reviewed and the responses were submitted to the National Half-Yearly Meeting. This new method allowed the national leaders to have a clear overview of the Society. The review was also a useful disciplinary device for the lower meetings because the submission of truthful answers meant that each individual would have to live up to the high moral standard created by the report or else negate the exercise. The Quaker preacher and school master, James Gough, thought in retrospect that elders and ministers should fulfil their duty and nip disorder in the bud. According to Gough, those young people who 'refused submission to good order' and 'whose tables abounded with elegant dishes and variety of liquor' fell into disgrace.[47]

Spiritual leaders, like Gough, had good cause for complaint because 1740 to 1760 was a period of great spiritual anxiety. The galleries were stripped of elders and ministers and the lack of representatives to the Half-yearly meeting indicated that there was indeed spiritual decline in the community.[48] Gough complained that many elders were making language and clothes the test of religion while their main interest was in financial reward.[49] Even so, a spiritual core remained intact. The National Meeting had to constantly remind the community to place value on spiritual rather than temporal blessings.[50]

Meanwhile the Methodist movement was beginning in Ireland. Friends generally did not perceive this new spiritual manifestation as threatening, but in a qualified manner welcomed it. One Quaker family in Cork entertained John Wesley with tea and loaned him a book of pious obituaries.[51] Wesley himself noted that a few Friends underwent water baptism, a sacramental test not recognised as a necessary part of faith by the Quakers.[52] However there does not seem to be any record of disownment over this. A public encounter between Irish Friends and the Methodists occurred in 1748. John Wesley, in

46 Jones, Later Periods, pp. 134–7. See also, Wight and Rutty, *History*, pp. 323–5.
47 James Gough, *Memoirs of the Life, Religious Experiences and Labours in the Gospel of ...* (Dublin, 1781), p. 106.
48 Yearly Meeting Minutes, x mo, 1755 and xi mo, 1736; John Rutty, *Spiritual Diary and Soliloquies* (London, 1796), p. 96.
49 Gough, *Memoirs*, p. 109.
50 Yearly Meeting Minutes, ix mo, 1750.
51 Frank Baker, *The Relations between the Society of Friends and Early Methodism* (London, 1949), p. 2n.
52 Nehemiah Curnock (ed), *Journal of John Wesley* (8 vols., London, 19??–??), iii, p. 27.

a sermon at Edenderry, attacked John Curtis, a Friend from Bristol, by accusing him of undermining his work. James Gough and other Quaker leaders
responded by seeking an interview with Wesley at Mountmellick. The consul-
tation produced an amiable result when Wesley accepted that his remarks
were ill-informed.[53]

Gough, like many Quakers, welcomed the Methodists and 'sincerely wished
the increase and promotion of solid piety'.[54] However, their chief criticism
was that the preachers made regeneration an instantaneous event for the
individual. They believed that overfamiliarity and excessive talking about
spiritual matters led to empty religiosity without reliance on Christ the inward guide. The same implication can be seen when the Welsh Quaker, James
Griffiths came in 1749, saying of the Methodists, 'no people are more at a loss
what to do with silence in meeting'.[55]

The most important question facing the eighteenth-century Quakers was
the function of the intellect in religion.[56] We have already seen how literature
was sometimes viewed as profane, atheistic and undermining Scripture. Like
the rest of the godly the 'deistical spirit' was seen as particularly dangerous as
it degraded the Scriptures and encouraged a 'do as you like morality'.[57] Friends,
however, did continue to explore philosophical ideas. The Ballitore Quaker,
Richard Shackleton, was sought out by Edmund Burke concerning Cartesian
philosophy which shows that there was intellectual and philosophical interest
in some Quaker circles.[58]

An important influence on the spirituality of eighteenth-century Irish
Friends was 'Quietist Piety'.[59] This brand of piety was imported from the
European continent and emphasised a spiritual openness to the Divine, rather
than intellectual speculation. It was natural for Irish Friends to find this piety
congenial because of their dislike of 'enthusiasm' and it was also a corrective
to their rigid ethical and group structures. James Gough translated many
French Quietist writers into English.[60] John Rutty, a Dublin physician and
Quaker, enjoyed reading spiritual works by Catholic writers such as Francis
Xavier and Thomas á Kempis.[61] He also had very good relations with John
Wesley and occasionally treated his physical ailments. Samuel Fuller's cata-

---

53 Gough, *Memoirs*, pp. 95–9.
54 Ibid., p. 99.
55 'Journal of John Griffiths' in *American Friends Library*, v, p. 371.
56 Jones, *Later Periods*, chapter seven, passim.
57 For remarks reported by John Churchman see, 'Friends Travelling' JFHS, p. 255.
58 Mary Shackleton, *Leadbeater Papers* (2 vols., London, 1862), ii, letter xvi.
59 For a standard treatment of Quietism see, Jones, *Later Periods*, chapters two and
    three.
60 Ibid., pp. 57–8n.
61 Rutty, *Spiritual Diary*, introduction, p. xiii, he also favorably mentions St Theresa on
    p. 263.

logue of stock in his bookshop indicates his spiritual diet was indeed wide. Beside the usual Quaker writers, like Penn and Barclay, his catalogue included *The Archbishop of Cambray's dissertation on Pure Love and directions for a Holy Life with an account of the Life and Writings of the Lady Guion* and George Whitefield's *Sermon on the Source of Saving Knowledge*.[62]

Nevertheless, spiritually attuned Irish Quakers believed that their society was decaying and declining during the eighteenth century. The minutes from Half-yearly Meeting report that Friends were engaging in the practice of 'drinking health's, gaming, frequenting play-houses, music meetings and other such diversions'.[63] Spiritual leaders believed that this behaviour was inconsistent with the 'grace and sobriety required by the professors of Christianity' and that the behaviour was 'a torrent of libertinism that rushes in and tends to lay waste the Christian testimony borne by their forefathers'.[64] Some Irish Friends saw themselves as a 'remnant' which was 'concerned for the welfare of Zion'. This self-proclaimed 'remnant' was mainly, but not exclusively, from the administrative elite who increasingly saw their role as a defensive and authoritarian one. They used Bible-based metaphors that were militaristic, keeping the camp clean and manning the walls to prevent breaches in discipline. Education took on greater importance when it became obvious that their youth were failing to understand the significance of central testimonies of the Society. This lack of understanding was making the demarcation between themselves and other Protestants ambiguous. These spiritual leaders had a loyalty to a way of life and worship, testimonies and dress, language and tradition, but most of all to their family (past and present) which they believed held the community together. The Irish Quakers, then as now, had developed a way of life rather than a dogmatic or credal identification.

By the middle of the eighteenth century a small band of young Quakers began working to spiritually revive the Society in Ireland. Their approach to spiritual renewal was more sedate than that of the Methodists. Some of the members of the band were Elizabeth Carleton, Samuel Neale, Mary Peisley and Richard Shackleton.[65] They emphasised administrative and disciplinary measures rather than 'enthusiasm'.

One of the foremost and powerful leaders in this group was Samuel Neale. His spiritual development illustrates a common pattern which is found in the spiritual journals of Friends in America or England. Consciousness of the fragility of life and spiritual sensitivity caused him to mend his ways. His apprenticeship in Dublin exposed him to the usual temptations faced by a

62 Bewley, *Narrative*, contains a catalogue of the stock of the bookseller Samuel Fuller.
63 Yearly Meeting Minutes, iii mo, 1751.
64 Ibid.
65 Shackleton, *Memoirs*, p. 15.

young man including a few Quaker ones. After his apprenticeship he went off like 'a man of the world' complete with a liveried servant. An unanticipated attendance at the 'First-day' meeting at Cork led to his hearing the ministry of Catherine Payton, a visiting English Friend. Her ministry confirmed his Quaker beliefs and he took up the 'plain dress' and 'plain language'. Spiritual openness and a deeper sensitivity to the inward state of others was part of his preparation for a wider ministry. His ministry took him far afield to Wales, England, Holland and also to America with frequent returns to Ireland.[66]

The same process was occurring in other young Quakers and the National Meeting continued to keep up its barrage of epistles which advised Friends to resist the temptations of the world. Mourning dress was even seen as a 'new mode of degeneracy'.[67] Part of the process of administrative reform was advocating the use of simple furniture and dissuading the use of artistic pictures in the home. In 1752 Meetings were requested to draw up membership lists.[68] The failure to involve the young was recognised and it was recommended that younger members assist older ones in the appointed family visits which were an important feature of the spiritual life of the community. Many times these family visits coincided with ministerial visits from preaching Friends who were travelling under 'concern'. In 1756 the National Meeting recommended early participation by both young men and women in administrative meetings.[69]

Visiting Friends were very instrumental in resolving some of the spiritual tension of the Irish Quakers. Some of the most prominent in the mid-eighteenth century were John Churchman from America, Samuel Fothergill (son of John) from England, and John Griffiths from Wales. Their outsider's perspective lent some authority to their recommendations. But sometimes this was not the case. When John Churchman visited the Lurgan meeting in Ulster he ran into difficulties. The meeting there tried to exclude him from the disciplinary meeting. His assertion of rights prevented his exclusion and ensured that business there was properly carried out.[70]

One of the most significant reforms in the eighteenth century was defining the standard for membership. The aged administrative elite realised they could not control the wide range of members so they chose to include them. From 1760 membership was determined on the basis of heredity and immediate commitment which allowed wider participation in the administrative

---

66 Samuel Neale, *Some Account of Lives and Religious Labours of Samuel Neale and Mary Neale* (London, 1845).
67 Yearly Meeting Minutes, v mo, 1732.
68 Ibid., xi mo, 1752.
69 Ibid., v mo, 1756.
70 'Journal of John Churchman' in *American Friends Library*, vi, pp. 218–19.

meeting.[71] Although authoritarian attitudes still persisted by leaving business in the hands of a few this reform opened the way for potential participation by all the members. In some respects reform also gave consensus a greater place, which had been the genius of the early movement. In another respect, defining the membership on the basis of heredity can be regarded as reneging on original Quaker insight. However, the motivation for making this choice was survival.

The process of reform was given a greater fillip in 1762. Samuel Fothergill, Jonathan Raines, Isaac Wilson and William Rathbone were appointed by the London Yearly Meeting to assist Irish Friends. These 'reformers' proceeded to each monthly meeting in Ireland with a set of queries. All those who 'professed', even those who were not in 'unity', were requested to remain after meeting to join in the exercise. The clerk of each business meeting was requested to read out the queries with the overseers making replies.[72] The focus of attention was on education, books, the role of parents, 'marrying out' and tithes. The significance of the visit of these London Friends was not so much in the questions or answers but in the group exercise of facing, in a spiritual or prayerful way, the reality of the state of their society. The National Meeting issued an epistle containing the results of this enquiry.[73] John Rutty noted favourably in his diary that the 'presbytery and ministry shone with splendour and surely the seed sown shall not be wholly lost'.[74]

III

The Quakers had moved on from their original state which was religiously and spiritually radical. Their administrative meetings allowed consensual structures to form which served the needs of their changing community. This creative leadership enable them to establish accommodation between themselves and the state along with the wider Irish community. The cost of accommodation, however, was curbing spiritual enthusiasm and radical agendas both social and political. As time passed Quakers had to adjust to new threats. Wealth naturally led to social acceptance and pressure to identify with their Protestant peers. But, their prosperity, along with endogamous marriage, also gave them the ability and opportunity to resist assimilation. The adoption of plain dress and language was another important factor in main-

---

71 Yearly Meeting Minutes, xi mo, 1760 and xi mo, 1762.
72 The procedures associated with the visit are described in Shackleton, *Memoirs*, pp. 33–4.
73 *An Epistle from the Friends who visited the Quarterly and Monthly Meetings of the Kingdom of Ireland in the Year 1762* (Dublin, 1762).
74 Rutty, *Diary*, p. 224.

taining their separate identity. Threats, both internal and external, to their community led to authoritarian attitudes among the elites in the administrative meeting which did not stop the numerical decline of the community. Some Quaker historians have blamed Quietist theology for their numerical demise, but it is more likely that given the spiritual circumstances of the eighteenth century, Quietist spirituality actually helped the Quakers to survive as a Christian community. Quietist piety also allowed them to retain some of their original radical spirituality. Quaker spirituality was never intellectually static but was part of a living spectrum. By the end of the seventeenth century their radical ideas were directed toward business innovation as a result of being stifled politically, which led to economic success. The chief problem for Irish Quakers during this period was the failure of their spiritual leadership to really lead their community. The leadership's problem lay not so much in their doctrine as in their wealth. Furthermore, the community's inward spirituality truncated a more creative engagement with the world.

The Less-favoured Refuge: Ireland's Nonconformist Huguenots at the Turn of the Eighteenth Century*

RAYMOND PIERRE HYLTON

'Suivant la discipline et la forme ancienne et ordinaire de nos eglises en France ...' [According to the discipline and the old and plain form of our churches in France]. These words were written with more than a slight touch of defiance. These were words penned by Huguenot pastors, not in France, under persecution, but in refuge—at Portarlington, in the Irish midlands. Insistent words, they appear in every burial entry of the French nonconformist church there from 1694 to 1702.[1] Moreover, there is something more than mere defiance, there is affirmation. In this instance the defiance is not directed solely at Louis XIV's militant popery, but at the more proximate threat of alleged Neo-Laudianism. The affirmation proclaims preservation of the old, unsullied faith, and keeping the torch of Coligny and Conde burning into the years of exile. Also, in its deeper meaning, it was the affirmation that the exiles would presently return to a cleansed and godly France, suitable for the elect. For the vast majority of these Huguenots, Ireland and other havens were viewed as temporary abodes; for Louis XIV would return to his senses and beckon home his Protestant subjects.[2] Nonconformity was one of the means by which many Huguenots could express and keep this hope alive.

In the past nonconformist exiles have been considered as the step-children of conformity in Huguenot studies. Historians and proto-historians have be-

---

* Dedicated to the memory of Miss Elizabeth Claire Strother, who left us on 14 March 1995 at the age of twenty-two, far before her time; but never beyond rememberance ... *A'bientot.*

1 The pastors were Jacques Gillet and Benjamin de Daillon. Portarlington, The Register of St Paul's (I would like to thank the rector, Dr Edward Woods, for his kind permission to view this manuscript); also printed in T.P. Le Fanu (ed), 'Registers of the French Church at Portarlington', *Proceedings of the Huguenot Society of London—Quarto Series*; xix (Aberdeen, 1908), pp. 2–36.

2 J-P Pittion, 'The French Protestants and the Edict of Nantes (1549–1685): A chronology based on material in Marsh's Library, Dublin', in C.E.J. Caldicott, H. Gough and J-P Pittion (eds), *The Huguenots and Ireland: anatomy of an emigration* (Dun Laoghaire, 1987), pp. 60–1.

trayed a distinct bias in favour of the conformist congregations. Until a relatively recent date, Huguenot nonconformists have been downplayed, or even ignored. When they have been discussed they have been portrayed as being stubborn and unrealistic, or worse, as ecclesiastical dinosaurs.[3] Certainly this interpretation may be partially explained by a predisposition on the part of many researchers to an Anglican orientation. Perhaps, also, it was not considered wise, in view of the vulnerable nature of the Irish Protestant community, to admit of substantial division within the Huguenot refuge.[4] The fact remains that the question of conformity versus nonconformity was an absorbing and often bitter issue with the Huguenot *diaspora*, an issue which was resolved only by default through the passage of time, and through assimilation.

It is not surprising that the Huguenot refuge was schizophrenic. From its inception, French Calvinism carried within itself the seeds of division. There had always existed among the Calvinistic community a more fundamental, uncompromising, often violent strain of 'zealot'.[5] In contradistinction there were also individuals, *politiques*, who were more willing under certain circumstances to bend, accommodate and compromise within the boundaries set by the power of worldly rulers, even if these rulers were considered to be idolatrous and apostate.[6] In Ireland there were three major periods of Huguenot immigration: the early Ormondite, 1662–9; the late Ormondite, 1681–7; and the Ruvignac, 1692–c.1706. These influxes were distinct, both in their composition and in the problems they posed for the Anglican establishment.[7]

---

3 D.C. Agnew, *Protestant exiles from France in the reign of Louis XIV* (London, 1877), pp. 106–7; E.D. Borrowes, 'The Huguenot Colony at Portarlington in Queen's County' in *Ulster Journal of Archaeology*, vi, no. 8 (1858), p. 328; J.C. Combe, 'The Huguenot's in the Ministry of the Church of Ireland', PhD thesis, Queen's University of Belfast, 1970, pp. 401, 405; James Floy, 'The Huguenot Settlement at Portarlington in *Proceedings of the Huguenot Society of London*, iii (London, 1892), pp. 16–17; S.J. Knox, *Ireland's debt to the Huguenots* (Dublin, 1959), p. 68; G.L. Lee, *The Huguenot settlements in Ireland* (London, 1936), pp. 148–9, 153, 227; T.P. Le Fanu, 'The Huguenot Church of Dublin and their Ministers.

4 Combe, 'The Huguenot's in the Ministry of the Church of Ireland', p. 406. The idea of dissension within the ranks of the French refugees did not fit well with the ideal of Protestant solidarity and the stereotype which later Anglophone writers bestowed upon the Huguenots, that they were models of sobriety, discipline, self-restraint and industrious. This image had been cultivated as early as the sixteenth century, and achieved is apotheosis in 1916 with the screening of the St Bartholomew's Day Massacre segment in D.W. Griffith's cinematic epic, *Intolerance*.

5 Daniel Ligou, *Le Protestantisme en France de 1598 a 1715* (Paris, 1968), p. 171.

6 Ibid., p. 175; Solange Deyon, *Du Loyalisme au Refus: les Protestants Francais et leur Depute-General entre la Fronde et la Revocation* (Lille, 1968), p. 91.

7 Robin Gwynn, 'Government Policy Towards Huguenot Immigration and Settlement in England and Ireland' in C.E.J. Caldicott, et al., *The Huguenots and Ireland*, pp. 211, 217–21.

The Church of Ireland after the Restoration was caught between a Catholic anvil and dissenting hammer. One of the priorities of James Butler, the duke of Ormond, after he became the Irish Lord Lieutenant in 1661, was strengthening the established church. Even if he had not been thus inclined, he would have fallen under strong pressure from the episcopal hierarchy and the secretary of state in London, Henry Hyde, earl of Clarendon, to do so. Ormond was deeply interested in attracting Huguenots and other foreign Protestants who had valuable skills beneficial to Ireland's economic development to come and settle.[8] Reconciling these two aims was not without pitfalls because French nonconformity and episcopal demands contained the potential for debilitating conflict. Therefore Ormond was deeply concerned about placing too many restrictions on the refuge's religious practices because to do so might remove incentives for them to come to Ireland thereby nullifying his economic projects which were based on foreign Protestant expertise. He adopted a formula of worship which was based on one developed in London by the French Church of the Savoy. This formula fit in well with Ormond's moderate policy and personality and gave him leeway to pursue Protestant immigration and placate aggressive Anglicans. His policy led to the establishment of the French Conformed Church of St Patrick's Cathedral, also known as 'French Patrick'. This Dublin congregation met for worship in the Lady Chapel in the cathedral.[9]

The latitude allowed these French worshippers was, in the Restoration context, considerable. Most significantly Ormond's formula made sure that there was no tampering with their cherished Calvinist ecclesiastical polity. What emerged was a paradoxical situation whereby the transplanted French Calvinist apparatus of an empowered consistory of pastors and elders, who exercised authority over the congregation's religious and social functions, existed under an Anglican canopy. Their style of worship retained the traditions of Theodore Beza, Abel Conrart, and Clement Marot with distinctive

8 J.C. Simms, 'The Restoration, 1660–1685' in T.W. Moody, F.X. Martin and F.J. Byrne, *A New History of Ireland* (Oxford, 1978), iii, p. 433; Maurice Craig, *Dublin, 1660–1860* (Dublin, 1980), pp. 3–4, 38; Richard Greaves, ' "That's no good religion that disturbs government": the Church of Ireland and the non-conformist challenge, 1660–88' in Alan Ford, James McGuire and Kenneth Milne (eds), *As by Law Established: the Church of Ireland since the Reformation* (Dublin, 1995), pp. 121–4; idem, '"Great Scott!", the Restoration in turmoil, or, Restoration crises and the emergence of party' in *Albion*, xxv (Winter, 1993) p. 608; Ormond's political career was linked to the earl of Clarendon and Clarendon's fall in 1667 led to Ormond's dismissal in 1669, James McGuire, 'Why was Ormond dismissed in 1669?' in *Irish Historical Studies*, xviii (March, 1973); Thomas Carte, *The Life of James, Duke of Ormond* (5 vols., London, 1736), v, p. 202; Lady Burghclare, *The Life of James, First Duke of Ormond, 1610–1688* (2 vols., London, 1912), ii, pp. 131–2.
9 T.P. Le Fanu, 'The Huguenot Churches of Dublin and their Ministers', p. 5; National Library of Ireland, MS 2678, p. 12.

Psalm-singing and the pastor's sermon remained central and of paramount importance. Most importantly a method for supporting the minister was devised initially by pluralism of benefices and later by stipend. What was asked in return was acceptance and utilisation of a French translation of the Book of Common Prayer, episcopal ordination and acknowledgment of the ultimate authority of the archbishop of Dublin.[10] The first condition engendered very little controversy. Long before the Restoration the consistory at Geneva, Switzerland had examined the Book of Common Prayer and discovered nothing objectionable. Also, there was a French translation readily available composed by Jean Durel.[11] However, episcopal ordination and authority were substantial stumbling blocks. Some worshippers accepted these religious innovations with good grace while others viewed them as the thin edge of the wedge, that would open the door to the gradual pollution of their faith.

The early Ormondite Huguenot refuge remained small and comparatively docile, and there was as yet no major or overt Calvinist-Anglican confrontation within the *Corps du Refuge* itself. It is doubtful that this early community numbered in excess of 500 individuals throughout Ireland. In Dublin, where there was the highest concentration, the majority originated in areas of France north of the River Loire (mainly Normandy). Significantly, Huguenot communities in northern France tended to be small, scattered and vulnerable. Therefore since the 1590s they had generally cultivated a low profile and were more accommodating with outsiders.[12] There is every indication that this translated into a more ready acceptance of conforming stipulations issued by the Church of Ireland, which, for all its flaws, was closer to Huguenot religion, both theologically and practically, than the Roman Catholic church. Even so, the facade began to fall off shortly after Ormond's dismissal in 1669. By 1672 the Refuge had dwindled considerably, and the French Patrick's congregation faced extinction. Out of twelve confirmed Huguenot families in Dublin, six had turned to nonconformity, though not in a separate French church. The unsubstantiated contemporary gossip that a French dissenting

10 Emile G. Leonard, *Histoire General du Protestantisme* (2 vols., Paris, 1961), ii, pp. 94, 317–18; Robin Gwynn, *Huguenot Heritage: the history and contribution of the Huguenots in Britain* (London, 1985), p. 99; T.P. Le Fanu, 'The Huguenot Churches of Dublin and their Ministers', pp. 6, 11; National Library of Ireland, MS 8007; J.J. Digges La Touche, 'Registers of the Conformed Churches of St Patrick's and St Mary's' in *Proceedings of the Huguenot Society of London—Quarto Series* (Aberdeen, 1893), vii, p. 1.

11 T.P. Le Fanu, 'The Huguenot Churches of Dublin and their Ministers', p. 5. Durel was originally a minister at Jersey. After removing to London he and Jacques Hierome were instrumental in establishing the French Church of the Savoy. Hierome later became the first pastor of 'French Patrick's' (1665–77).

12 David Parker, 'Huguenots in seventeenth-century France' in A.C. Hepburn (ed), *Minorities in History* (London,, 1978), p. 14; Deyon, *Du Loyalisme au Refus*, p. 161.

congregation was meeting at the house of the wife of Ormond's nephew, Lady Ossory, is too far-fetched to merit credence, particularly in view of the Butler family's staunch support for the Church of Ireland.[13]

The late Ormondite influx, following upon the Dragonnades of 1681, was a larger migration. This group also proved to be less manageable than their predecessors. The majority of these refugees were not merchants and originated south of the River Loire where Huguenot congregations tended to be larger. In many of these areas they were substantial, or even predominate, part of the local population, such as Poitou, Aunis, Saintonge, Languedoc and Dauphine. The factor of intimidation was therefore not as pronounced in shaping their attitude to outsiders. These southern Huguenots were much more traditional and less inhibited in their resistance to compromise and conformity.[14] During the tense summer of 1683 the first documented attempt at establishing a nonconforming French congregation occurred. It was at this time that the Rye House Plot was attempted in England and Ormond was convinced that the plotters had an Irish tentacle in the Protestant dissenting community. At this juncture a French minister named (Jean?) Jacques, abetted by a fan maker (Pierre?) Leroux, along with a Dutch painter began luring members away from French Patrick's to join English-speaking conventicles. The earl of Arran, deputising for his father, and acting with the assent of the conformist pastor, Moise Viridet, forcibly broke up the conventicles and on several occasions arrested the three ringleaders which forced them to leave Ireland. Soon after another nonconforming Huguenot minister appeared in Dublin and attempted to solicit potential members after common prayer for the purpose of organising a nonconforming meeting. He too was forced to flee Ireland. Though nonconforming sentiment obviously existed there is no evidence that Huguenot nonconformists assembled regularly; contrary statements must, on the basis of current research, be considered apocryphal.[15] However the lesson from the Rye House fiasco was apparently learned. Huguenot nonconformists became aware that if they wanted to parade their nonconformity they were better advised to do so on their own and avoid any taint of association with English-speaking dissenters, especially Presbyterians. The authorities did in fact discriminate among the varieties of dissent. Hu-

---

13 *Calendar of State Papers, Domestic*, xxviii; Addenda 1660–1685, pp. 363–4; Thomas Gimlette, *The History of the Huguenot settlers in Ireland and other literary remains* (Waterford, 1888), pp. 199, 273.

14 David Parker, 'Huguenots in seventeenth-century France', p. 23; Ligou, *Le Protestantisme en France*, p. 161.

15 Ormond arrested the miscreant pastor in London, but released him. Historical Manuscripts Commission, *Calendar of the manuscripts of the marquess of Ormonde* (new series, 11 vols., London, 1895–1920) vii, pp. 65, 81, 89, 93–5, 104, 106, 108–9, 139, 150, 155; J.S. Reid, *The History of the Presbyterian Church in Ireland* (2nd edn, 3 vols., Belfast, 1867), ii, 464–5.

guenot dissenters, due to their comparative small numbers and the sympathy they engendered by their suffering and persecution in France, held a relatively favoured position in comparison to other Protestant dissenting societies, although not officially tolerated, were generally not harassed by the national government. As long as Huguenot dissenters maintained their distinctive character they benefited from this reservoir of good will. This, however, never elevated their official status to a level of equality with their conformist brethren.[16]

The Jacobite interlude and subsequent Williamite establishment brought about substantial changes in direction for the Irish Huguenot refuge. The post-1692 situation was unprecedented and unique. At this stage the most substantial Huguenot migration took place and was led by Henri de Massue, second Marquis de Ruvigny and later Lord Galway. He provided a focal point for the refuge which had hitherto been lacking and became the ultimate *Depute-General* of the French Calvinist Church (*Religion Pretendu Reforme*). Of critical importance, however, as far as nonconformity was concerned, was the passage of the 1692 Act of the Irish Parliament 'for encouraging Protestant strangers to settle and plant in Ireland'. This statute went much further towards toleration than any previous one; nonconformity was implicitly permitted which distinctively marked the end of the Ormondite era.[17]

Nonconformist sentiment was more pronounced among the new arrivals with about two-thirds embracing it. As a result an independent congregation was organised in Dublin and met in accommodation rented from Councillor Thomas Whitshed on Bride Street. This new congregation also purchased a tenant's interest of £16 in a burial plot near the north side of St Stephen's Green. This spectacular resurgence of old-style Calvinism so alarmed the consistory of French Patrick's that they petitioned Lord Galway to arrange some sort of accommodation. This led Galway to summon Jacques Severin a pastor who was serving in London at that time. After his arrival in Dublin Severin opened dialogue with the consistory of the dissenting congregation in Bride Street headed by their pastors; Barthelemy Balaquier and Joseph Lagacherie. Severin drew up articles of union in April 1693 and both of the French congregations voted on receiving them. French Patrick's accepted the articles but the nonconformists overwhelmingly and emphatically rejected them. Because the articles have not survived the exact points of contention are open to speculation. However, to contemporaries the issues were significant enough to create bitter and divisive attitudes in the Huguenot community.

16 Genealogical Office, Dublin, MS 4, pp. 147–54; J.C. Beckett, *Protestant Dissent in Ireland, 1687–1784* (London, 1948), pp. 127.
17 Deyon, *Du Loyalisme au Refus*, pp. 150–60; The previous act 'for encouraging Protestant strangers never admitted the possibility of toleration for dissenters, Cf. 14–15 Charles II c xiii and 4 William and Mary c 2.

Also, the matter was serious enough that Galway had to take the extraordinary step of calling together prominent members of both congregations. At this meeting he personally implored them to live together in peace as 'Brethren', and to continue to search for other ways whereby they might unite. Afterward Galway used his prestige and diplomatic powers to persuade the parties to avoid controversy. He wanted to protect the Huguenot community from the danger of vitriolic flare-ups that would not only embarrass the exiles but would render political aid and comfort to those outside their community, in Ireland as well as Britain, who were pro-Catholic in sentiment. As it proved the tone was set for an often uneasy co-existence within the *Corps de Refuge* in Ireland between those adhering to Calvinist and Anglican tendencies.[18] Although the rival parties sometimes did on occasion co-operate with one another, and were at times even friendly, the underlying ethos was antagonistic with occasional venomous outbursts which broke through their sullen facade of silence.[19]

Nonconformity, however, was not confined to Dublin, though it was there and at Cork that it prevailed the longest. There were other noncomformist congregations which flourished for shorter periods of time at Carlow, Waterford, Lisburn and Portarlington. Portarlington witnessed the most serious Calvinist-Anglican confrontation in the Irish Huguenot community that is documented. Provisions in the 1700 Act of Resumption gave the bishop of Kildare, William Moreton, the leverage to impose conformity upon the French congregation under the guise of offering to consecrate the church building. Pastor Benjamin de Daillon resisted Moreton's directive which led the bishop to appoint the more pliable Antione Ligonier de Bonneval as a replacement pastor there. As a result a schism lasting six years dragged on with its effects lasting much longer. A slight majority in the congregation supported Daillon, who continued to preside over the consistory, to the bedevilment of Bonneval. Eventually Daillon relocated to Carlow where he officiated at the nonconforming French church there.[20] Moreton's version of events (the only version that is

---

18 T.P. Le Fanu, 'The Huguenot Churches of Dublin and their Ministers', pp. 17–18, 26, 253; Marsh's Library, Dublin, MS Z4.3.20; National Library of Ireland, MS 8007.

19 There were lingering controversies between conformists and nonconformists within Huguenot congregations in Portarlington and Cork. Jacques Fontaine, *Memoires d'une famille Huguenote, victimes de la Revocation de l'Edit de Nantes* (Toulouse, 1877), pp. 241–9.

20 National Archives, Dublin, Ref. 2/447/17; 25/2/1740; 2/3/1788; 2/447/13; 25/11/1745; 4/11/1774; 26/3/1796 (I owe these references to the kindness of Vivien Costello); *Calendar of State Papers, Domestic, 1696*, p. 6; National Library of Ireland, microfilm p. 4531, p. 70; Borrowes, 'The Huguenot Colony at Portarlington in Queen's County', p. 328; Lee, Huguenot Settlements, p. 152; Agnew, *Protestant Exiles from France in the Reign of Louis XIV*, p. 107; *Formulaire de la Consecracion et Dedicace des Eglises et Chapelles selon l'usage de l'Eglise d'Irlande* (Dublin, 1702).

extant) fosters the belief that the controversy focused on Daillon's consistorial authority. However this was just a subterfuge because the issues were more complex and the religious principles at stake ran far deeper than polity for the Huguenots. Otherwise why was the split so long-lived and bitter? Also, what would have possessed over one hundred adults to place their signatures on a petition affirming their support for Daillon? The imposition of conformity at Portarlington was clumsy and was achieved at considerable cost to the refuge. It was the prime factor causing the Huguenot colony to decline demographically after 1702. Later, in the 1730s, the French community in Portarlington experienced further stress when crypto-dissent mingled with apocalyptic ideas which centred around the town's most eminent refuge, the Camisard prophet or cheiftain Jean Cavallier.[21]

The Anglican-Dissenter conflict was a very serious problem for the exiled French community wherever they went. In the North American colonies the conflict was similar, but sometimes lethal. In 1700 at Manakin Town, west of Richmond, Virginia, Huguenots with Irish connections established a settlement. This community was plagued by rancorous exchange of protest, threats and intimidation between the refugees and Royal authorities over conformity which continued on and off for years. In South Carolina a more serious situation developed at the Huguenot settlements of St James Santee and St Denis. In 1715 the Santee pastor, Phillipe de Richebourg, openly rejected Jean Durel's translation of the Book of Common Prayer. The crisis was exacerbated and escalated when charismatic Cevenol prophets, Jean Dutartre and Pierre Rombert, arrived. Shortly after, in 1724, open revolt ensued with the loss of life and subsequent executions. In this context the importance of schism in the early eighteenth-century French Protestant community in Ireland should not be denied or even underestimated.[22]

Determining who these French dissenters were is somewhat problematic because only the Dublin and Cork congregations endured for an appreciable length of time. Also, the congregational registers of the Cork contingent have not survived. Presently only Dublin can be evaluated, and that under limitations. Though nonconforming Huguenots were more numerous their records are not as complete as their conforming brethren, especially of French Patrick's and French Mary's, and what survives contain large gaps. Another contribut-

---

21 *Formulaire de la Consecracion et Dedicace*; R.P. Hylton, 'The Huguenot Settlement at Portarlington, 1692–1771' in C.E.J. Caldicott, et al., *The Huguenots and Ireland:*, pp. 311–13; Maurice Pezet, *L'Epopee des Camisards* (Paris, 1978), p. 194; Agnew, *Protestant Exiles from France in the Reign of Louis XIV*, p. 64.

22 Jon Butler, *The Huguenots in America: a refugee people in New World society* (Cambridge, 1983), pp. 116–17, 119, 217–19. For Cevenol prophets see, Hillel Schwartz, *The French Prophets: the history of a millenarian group in eighteenth-century England* (Berkeley, 1980).

ing factor is that many sources have been destroyed as a result of burglary and vandalism.[23]

Two salient factors about the nonconforming community in the early eighteenth century are worthy of note. Insofar as figures on provincial origins may be discerned; the vast majority of families came from the southern sector of the 'Huguenot Crescent': 47 from Aunis and Saintonge; 45 from the Languedoc; 29 from Guyenne; and 9 from Poitou. Even though nearly all social classes, economic circumstances, trades, calling and professions are represented in the French dissenting community the proportion of aristocratic families is striking. Out of 419 surnames, 92 are definitely from noble families, which amount to more than one in five families being of very high social status.[24] This constituency of noble families certainly was a significant factor in the longevity of the nonconforming community in Dublin. In the North America settlements French dissenting communities collapsed with incredible rapidity in every colony where they settled after the 1720s.[25] In Dublin the strength of the nonconforming community depended on two factors. This community had a natural leadership in the *noblesse d'epee* [noble families] who acted as a visible reservoir for traditional values and served as an example to those in lower social status. Another factor was that these nobles received fervent support from the members in their respective local nonconforming congregations, whose southern French orientation made them far less intimidated by the Church of Ireland hierarchy. Furthermore these nonconformists were undaunted in their hope of living to see a reversal of fortune that would eventually led to a return to France.

Although Lord Galway was a focal point of political authority for the French refugees in Ireland he was not universally respected within the greater Huguenot community, and less so among the dissenters. Even though he, along with his conformist circle, wielded considerable political power and influence the French exiles repeatedly rebuked his attempts to mediate and unite the community. There was by no means a scenario of unquestioning adulation for him which was rooted in his prior career in France. He and his father had been Deputes-General and many believed that they had evinced a quasi-sacrilegious loyalty to the crown. There were considerable hard feelings that remained over their delivering a Huguenot zealot, Roux de Marcilly, over to the royal executioner. Also, many believed that they had been too passive

23 David Dickson, 'Huguenots in the urban economy of eighteenth-century Dublin and Cork' in E. Caldicott, et al., *The Huguenots and Ireland*, pp. 322–3; The registers of the French Non-Conformist Churches of Lucy Lane and Peter Street, Dublin, T.P. Le Fanu (ed) in *The Publications of the Huguenot Society of London* (Aberdeen, 1901), xiv, p. xii.

24 British Library, London, Additional MS 9718, pp. 35–508.

25 Butler, *The Huguenots in America*, pp. 40, 77, 92, 107, 199, 211.

in response to the Dragonades and persecutions in the early 1680s that led to the Revocation in 1685. As a result, in the eyes of many in both the conforming and nonconforming community, especially those holding a zealot or apocalyptic religion his word was not to be trusted. There was further resentment of Galway because he did not achieve the desired goal of returning to France in the part he played in the treaties of Ryswick and Utrecht. When Galway died in 1720 there was no real enthusiasm within the French Dispersion to replace him in his role as a political leader.[26]

In 1697, Dublin's nonconforming Bride Street congregation split into two. On the northside a meeting was formed on the west-side of Lucy Lane near Chancery Place. The other group moved to rented accommodation in Wood Street. Though these cells continued to be governed by the same consistory the Wood Street members seceded in 1701 over the issue of an additional pastoral appointment. In 1707 there was a reconciliation and reunification with the Lucy Lane congregation. Shortly after the southside worshippers moved to permanent meeting site, complete with a burial ground, on Peter Street which came to be known as 'French Peter's'. As the eighteenth century progressed the Lucy Lane membership dwindled resulting in a physical merger with French Peter's in 1773. In turn French Peter's itself was forced to close for worship in 1814. However, some degree of consistorial administration remained over the property and use of the cemetery continued for some decades thereafter.[27]

The fissure between those willing to conform and those more dedicated to Calvinist doctrine and practice was sometimes really a political ploy. For instance, the temporary secession of the French Mary congregation from French Patrick is a most glaring example. After French Patrick had grown substantially a significant portion of the congregation began to met north of the Liffey in the old chapter house of St Mary's Abbey on Meetinghouse Lane. The issue occasioning the rupture occurred on 5 January 1705 and was over clerical seniority rather than doctrine. Even though nonconformity was not really an issue in the split there was a proposal to unite the French Mary meeting with the Lucy Lane temple which engendered much vituperation, but was never a serious proposal. The leader of this quasi-schism, Pastor Pierre Peze de Galiniere, was employing a bit of political blackmail in order to secure a government subsidy for the salary of his assistant Pascal Ducasse. De Galiniere and the French Mary consistory deliberately sabotaged the merger

26 J.S. Reid, *The History of the Presbyterian Church in Ireland*, p. 458; Deyon, *Du Loyalisme au Refus*, pp. 9, 27–8, 92, 96–7, 159–60; Ligou, *Le Protestantisme en France*, pp. 74–5; Pezet, *L'Epopee des Camisards*, p. 83; Charles Lart, 'The Huguenot Regiments' in Proceedings of the Huguenot Society of London, Vol. ix, p. 472.

27 The registers of the French Non-Conformist Churches, pp. v, xi, 34, 85; T.P. Le Fanu, 'The Huguenot Churches of Dublin and their Ministers', p. 20.

by attaching the approval of the archbishop of Dublin, William King, as a precondition for agreement. Also, the advantage of remaining under the Church of Ireland umbrella was just too cozy to jeopardise at the expense of pursuing a nostalgic vision.[28]

The distinctive character of Huguenot religion and worship was derived in large part from the exclusive use of French as their liturgical language. Due to being a linguistic as well as a religious minority there was a necessity and a practical sense to employ the language of their host country. However, it was equally logical, since they might at any time be able to return to France, to preserve the traditional liturgical forms, expressed in the inviolate purity of the ancestral tongue. Hence, long after reason or necessity had passed, the persistent rendering of church registers and consistory minutes in French was a hallmark of Irish Huguenot congregations. Sometimes this resulted in odd or even humorous renditions of those with Irish and English surnames recorded as godparents or spouses.[29]

Their adherence to linguistic purity went hand-in-hand with their Calvinist reverence for the unadulterated precepts which they believed were contained within the Bible. The intent to follow, to as great a degree as possible, the direct words of Divine inspiration led their shunning composed hymns in favour of the singing of Psalms from the Old Testament during and sometimes outside of church services.[30] It is indeed indicative of this sense of reverence that the weekly Huguenot worship services, held on Sunday afternoons, always began with psalm-singing. For this purpose, French-language Psalters were used in place of hymnals. On occasion a 'toner' was selected from the congregation to sing out the first verse which was followed in unison by the rest of the worshippers. Another feature of their worship was that musical instruments were not to be used at service.[31]

Within the French Dispersion there were a number of Psalms which were very popular. Psalms that conveyed the theme of supplication in the face of adversity and impending despair followed by the hope of deliverance were especially embraced. The pangs of exile made Psalm 137, the song of the Judean captives in Babylon, of singular poignancy in regard to the French communities in exile because of their identification with the example of the heartbroken Jews longing to return to Jerusalem. This type of sentiment intertwined with millenarian ideas amongst Huguenot dissenters who tended

28 G.A. Forrest, 'Schism and Reconciliation: the Nouvelle Eglise de Ste Marie, Dublin, 1705–16' in Proceedings of the Huguenot Society of Great Britain and Ireland, vol. xxvi, no. 2, 1995; Historical Manuscripts Commission, *Second Report*, appendix, p. 243; National Library of Ireland, MS 8007.

29 'Queli' for Kelly and 'Magwire' for McGuire are two examples.

30 A.J. Grant, *The Huguenots* (Hamden, Connecticut, 1969), p. 72; Robin Gwynn, *Huguenot Heritage* (London, 1985), pp. 21, 24, 98.

31 Grant, p. 73.

to envision King William III as a modern–day King Cyrus who had facilitated the return of the Jews to their homeland.[32] Therefore, just as in the case of the ancient Jews, it was very necessary to maintain the purity of their faith and to conscientiously adhere to its forms. This particular religious practice showed that they were prepared to endure the test of suffering and that they had a continual faith in their eventual redemption. The ghastly violence expressed in the last verse of Psalm 137 also shows the reality of their embittered exile and their vengeful militancy which was rooted in their foundation during the 1550s and 60s. Militant sentiment led many individuals, both conformed and dissenting, to actively engage in supporting the wars against their former sovereign, Louis XIV. Both religious groups were dominated by the *noblesse d'epee* many of whom engaged in actual combat during the several wars of the late seventeenth and early eighteenth centuries. As a result many received pensions from the English and Irish establishments and were called back and forth to the wars.[33] Within the dissenting community there were a number of leaders from military nobility such as: Jacques de Belrieu, Baron de Virazel at Dublin; Josias de Robillard de Champagne, Daniel le Grand Du Petit Bosc, Robert d'Ully, Vicomte de Laval at Portarlington; and Pierre de Franquefort at Waterford. Such a leadership undoubtedly strengthened the dissenters' resolve to bend as little as possible to the exigencies of their new environment. Worship in Psalms was followed by spontaneous prayer which was in clear opposition to the reading of a prescribed formula for prayer. Dissenters rejected Durel's *Liturgie* as being contrived and artificial. Scripture reading, selected by their pastor and interspersed throughout the service, supervened prayer.

At weddings, the marriage ceremony was performed after prayers and Scripture readings, but before the sermon, so that the congregation was able to concentrate more fully and thus derive more benefit from the minister's message. Religious practice in relation to marriage required that the bride and groom be announced to the congregation from the pulpit for three consecutive Sundays. If there were no valid objections were put forward the ceremony could proceed. The rigid application of this formula in the French churches led to couples who wished a speedier process to marry in other Protestant chapels.[34]

The true ceremonial focal point of the worship service was not Communion, but the sermon. Much to the surprise of many outside observers nonconforming ministers delivered their sermons while wearing a hat. Like-

32 H. Bots and R. Bastiannse, 'Le refuge Huguenot et les Provinces-Unies: une equisse sommaire' in M. Magdelaine and R. von Thadden, *Le Refuge Huguenot* (Paris, 1985), p. 75.

33 *Hiberniae Notitis* (Dublin, 1723).

34 *Proceedings of the Parish Registers Society of Ireland*, xi, pp. 10–14, 19, 21, 24–8, 90–1, 95, 97; xii, pp. 9, 58, 72.

wise male members of the congregation wore headgear during worship. They only doffed their hats at certain solemn moments which did not include the administration of holy communion.[35] Conforming French ministers delivered their sermons wearing a surplice while dissenters refused this liturgical device and making the sign of the cross. But perhaps the greatest difference between conformists and nonconformists lay in the fact that sermonising from notes was forbidden to dissenting preachers. The preacher's words were to flow freely by Divine inspiration, so that God's admonitions were channelled directly to the congregation through the minister. Thus the sermon was in a crucial sense the most sacred moment in worship. The instance most closely approximated a direct communication from the Creator to his faithful. Therefore, yawning or sleeping, or being otherwise inattentive, during the sermon was considered an act of the utmost disrespect, punishable by consistorial censure.[36] It was virtually mandatory that all sermons be lengthy. The minimum length was an hour but it was rare that sermons lasted more than two hours. There was an expectation that the delivery would be spirited and evangelical. When John Wesley heard Gaspar Caillard preach at Portarlington he was very impressed by his animated style.[37]

Once every month the evening sermon was followed by holy communion. Fellowship at the communion service was restricted by the use of the *mareaux*, special tokens made of lead. The tokens were distributed by the pastor to the head of each household the Thursday prior to Communion Sunday. It was important to insure that all partakers be recognised as worthy. During the transitional period of their refugee situation when newcomers were arriving daily off the boat, so to speak, it was particularly difficult to regulate communion without tight control. French Catholic spies were in evidence masquerading, under a logical cover, as Huguenots. However, the prime consideration seems to have been to make certain that arriving French Calvinists publicly acknowledge any lapses in faith they had made under pressure in France. Therefore they had to demonstrate true repentance and be officially readmitted to the fold before they could receive the *mareaux*.[38] The process was known as 'reconaissance'. When people received communion the mareaux was presented and they received the elements standing with the men having their heads covered. Laymen, usually elders, assisted the pastor in distribution.

Necessity compelled the church of the Huguenot dispersion to initiate

35 Grant, p. 72.
36 In New England sleeping or yawning during the sermon was punished by law. John E. Pomfret and Floyd M. Shumway, *Founding the American Colonies* (New York, 1970), pp. 174–7; John C. Miller (ed), *Colonial Images* (New York, 1962), pp. 175–178.
37 The Journal of John Wesley, MA, Nehemiah Churnock, ed. (8 vols., London, 1909), ii, pp. 194–5
38 Historical Manuscripts Commission, *Report 15*, appendix, p. 53; Non-Conformist Church Registers, pp. 103–15; Gwynn, p. 181.

three unique ceremonial procedures which were customarily administered after communion. They were: *Reconnaissance*, *Abjuration* and *Reception*. *Reconnaissance* was designed to provide a conscientious avenue of forgiveness to
French Calvinists who had succumbed to persecution in France and who had
temporarily given lip-service conversion to the Roman Catholic church before
they made their escape. Beginning with the 1681 Dragonnades at Poitou, the
level of pressure and persecution had reached such a level of intensity and
pervasiveness that the vast majority of Huguenots had abjured. Far more had
remained in France as nominal Catholics, *Nouveaux Convertis*, than the esti-
mated 200,000 who actually fled abroad.[39] As opportunities for escape presented themselves refugees trickled in to Ireland (the penalty for attempting
an escape was life imprisonment in the galleys).[40] Therefore, it was necessary
to provide a vehicle wherein these people could cleanse themselves of the
abjuration. It was advantageous to have relatives and/or friends in the congregation to vouch for them. If not the process of *Reconnaissance* could take
longer. In Dublin, the length of time varied from as little as three weeks after
arriving from France to as long as six months.[41]

In every instance it was necessary for a lapsed Huguenot to place themselves in the charge of a minister. The minister questioned them about their
faith and circumstances. The repentant had to demonstrate the veracity of
their claims and their repentance had to be sincere. After receiving further
religious instruction the penitents had to 'come forward' before the congregation to explain and renounce the nature of their transgressions and express
their desire to return to the true faith. If the performance was deemed satisfactory those that had temporarily deviated were readmitted into the fellowship. The most frequently confessed sin was having assisted in the 'idolatrous
cult' of the Roman Church. On rarer occasions the offence was, due to their
not having the opportunity to flee, not keeping their obligation of divine
worship in the Reformed service.[42]

Closely connected to, but not identical with the *Reconaissance* was the
process of *Abjuration* by which a French Catholic renounced the Roman
Church and was officially received into the Huguenot communion. Many
times the parents of these individuals had been Protestants and on coming to
Ireland they were free to worship in their family tradition.[43] The abjurors, like
the candidates in *Reconaissance*, all appear to have been young adults in their
early twenties and natives of the provinces of Guyenne and Saintonge. Just
like those in *Reconaissance* pastors provided religious instructions before they

39 P. Joutard, '1685, une fin et une nouvelle chance pour le Protestantisme Français' in
   M. Magdelaine and R. von Thadden, pp. 13–14.
40 Gwynn, p. 91.
41 Non-Conformist Church Registers, pp. 103–15.
42 Ibid., p. 104.   43 Ibid., p. 105–15.

were received into the religious community. In one instance, Jacques Chretien in 1728, spousal influence played a decisive factor for on the same day that Jacques abjured the Roman Catholic religion, his wife Jeanne made her *Reconaissance*.[44]

The ceremony of *Reception* occurred when someone of who was not French wished to join a Huguenot congregation. Those seeking to join were examined by the pastor in relation to faith and moral conduct, first in private, and then before the consistory and congregation prior to acceptance into fellowship. The only recorded Reception in Dublin was when a Palatine, Jean Marlande, '*natif de Weissembourg en Allemagne*' applied.[45]

Irish Huguenots preferred to call their meeting houses '*eglises*' rather than the formerly used 'temple'. Their meeting houses lacked stained glass, steeples, outside crosses, high altars, statues and pictures. They were architecturally unadorned, boasting a plain rectangular shape with a classical gable; as in the postulated rendition of the Portarlington church prior to it remodelling into Victorian Gothic during the 1850s.[46]

The *Grande Catechisme* of pre-exillic Huguenot worship did not import well; and it must be said that its use was already fading in many regions of France before the revocation. When it was used it was after the evening sermon. The pastor employed the catechism to address questions to the congregation, particularly the elders, on matters of biblical interpretation and doctrines of faith.[47]

Millenarian ideas were pervasive and recurring factors within the Huguenot diaspora, particularly among those refugees who adhered more closely to the dissenting rather than conforming tradition. Although exillic millenarian ideas have been traditionally linked with theological differences arising among those who followed the piety of Pierre Jurieu and Pierre Bayle there is some evidence that there was a similar philosophical confrontation in the late seventeenth-century Irish Refuge.[48] At that time there was an unprecedented number of refugees from the southern provinces of France. These refugees streamed into Dublin , Portarlington, Cork and Waterford via the Swiss Cantons, Frankfurt-am-Main, the Netherlands and Britain. They brought with them apocalyptic ideas that threatened orthodox Calvinist theology. These Huguenots from southern France were in contrast to their northern counterparts from lower social classes. The wooded mountains of the regions of Cevennes and Vivarais in Languedoc were the only areas in France that the Calvinists were able to supplant the pagano-folk Catholicism of the French peasantry. In

44 Ibid., p. 113.
45 Ibid., p. 114.
46 See Knox, *Ireland's debt to the Huguenots* for a hypothetically reproduced illustration.
47 Grant, pp. 72–3.
48 Gwynn, p. 221.

the south the Huguenot religion was popular and evangelical which was transformed by unrelenting persecution into a militant apocalyptic religion and became known as Camisards.[49]

Within the Dutch, British and Irish Refuges apocalyptic sentiment was nurtured by atrocity reports filtering out of France and the Williamite victories in Ireland. King William himself was looked upon by them as messianic figure and many times was portrayed, both symbolically and literally as the liberator of Protestants. The Nine Years War evoked the hopeful image of King William leading the Grand Protestant Coalition (in which Huguenot regiments with veteran of the War of the Two Kings were to participate) fanned these expectations. The Ryswick negotiations dashed the hopes of an early return to France when Louis XIV flatly refused to consider any moderation of his religious policy.[50] In spite of these developments millenarian ideas did not abate but became more pervasive. Their ideas spread in an informal fashion and took the form of Nostrodamic prophecy. Some prophecies predicted the cataclysmic destruction of the Papacy and the complete moral redemption of the French monarchy.[51]

Millenarian ideas peaked during the Spanish War of Succession and there was a further rejuvenation during the Camisard War in Languedoc. The wars led to an exhaulted variety Cevenol apocalyptic visions which were expressed most notably by the French Prophets in London in the first decade of the eighteenth century.[52] The Prophets, who ultimately encompassed a far larger English-speaking element, were known for their visionary or charismatic religiosity. Speaking in tongues and alleged miracle-working was attributed to them. The movement made very little headway in the Irish Huguenot community in comparison to Britain and South Carolina. Its exhibitionist nature elicited a cold response from even nonconformist worshipers.[53] Their most celebrated figure in Ireland was the exiled Camisard leader Jean Cavallier. Although he admittedly spoke in tongues and prophesied while in the Cevennes while he was in Ireland he cultivated a air of respectability due to his marriage into a noble family.[54]

The prevalence of Socinian and other anti-Trinitarian doctrines is difficult to ascertain. Certainly the French Protestant communities in Britain and

---

49 Maurice Pezet, *Lepopee des Camisards* (Paris, 1978); Philippe Joutard, *Les Camisards* (Paris, 1976); Charles Taylor, *The Camisards* (London, 1893); Jean Cavallier, *Memoires of the Wars of the Cevennes* (Dublin, 1726).
50 Schwartz, *The French Prophets.*
51 Ibid., pp. 54, 60–81.
52 Ibid., pp. 125–6; Raymond P Hylton, The Huguenot Settlement at Portarlington, 1692–1771, MA thesis, National University of Ireland, University College Dublin, 1982, pp. 45–6, 105–6.
53 Portarlington Church register, pp. 36–97.
54 Cavllier, pp. i–xxiv.

Holland faced such doctrinal threats at the turn of the eighteenth century.[55] Therefore it does seem likely that Ireland was not exempt. Two nonconforming pastors Jean-Pierre Droz of Dublin and Gaspard Caillard who served in Dublin and Portarlington both had Socinian tendencies.[56]

The greater segment of the Huguenot refuge, however, had merely a nostalgic millenarian vision as the whole point of their worshipping community. They saw their suffering as the price to be paid for their faith. Therefore many thought that compromising, or even denial of their dreams, was a price that would render their exile meaningless. The actual outward form of worship between dissenters and conformists differed little. Nonconformists did not employ Durel's liturgy and their pastors and consistories generally demonstrated a lesser degree of flexibility in regard to ecclesiastic procedure.[57] Despite their differences there was some degree of cooperation between the rival doctrinal tendencies in the *Corp du Refuge*. They cooperated in charitable endeavours, exchanged ministers and even tacitly agreed to support one another in disciplining miscreants. Individual bequests were often willed with open hands to both conforming and dissenting churches; and many prominent members moved quite freely and amicably between both traditions. The permanent nature of the schism, however, belies any attempt to exaggerate the goodwill and sense of solidarity that did exist in the hearts of individuals.

Long after the dream of returning to France lost its claim to reality nonconformity continued. After some time Huguenot exiles did become Anglo-Irishmen of French extraction, but exactly when is a debatable point. As a result it is difficult to discern when the momentum of custom and tradition took on a greater relevance than their original religious convictions.

55 Gwynn, *Huguenot Heritage*, pp. 105–6.
56 Gaspar Caillard, *Sermons sur divers textes de lEcritude Sainte* (Dublin, 1728); Portarlington Church register, pp. 10, 16–17.
57 Burrowes, 'The Huguenot Colony at Portarlington in Queen's County', p. 33; Agnew, *Protestant Exiles from France in the Reign of Louis XIV*, p. 71.

The Reverend John Abernethy:
The Challenge of New Light Theology to
Traditional Irish Presbyterian Calvanism

R. FINLAY HOLMES

On 24 June 1720, the Synod of Ulster, meeting in Belfast unanimously approved an overture, appointing ministers 'who are members of this Synod'

> to preach Catechetick Doctrine, insisting on the great and fundamental Truths of Christianity, according to the Westminster Confession of Faith, and Catechisms, founded on the Holy Scriptures, such as the Being and Providence of God, and the Divine Authority of the Holy Scriptures; the necessary doctrine of the Ever Blessed Trinity in the unity of the Godhead, particularly the Eternal Deity of Our Lord Jesus Christ, as being of the same substance with the Father, and equal in power and glory: and of the satisfaction made to Divine justice, who is our only propitiation; of Regeneration by Efficacious Grace; of free justification by the Righteousness of our Lord Jesus Christ, received by Faith alone; of Original Sin; of the Morality of the Sabbath; the necessity of a holy life in order to the obtaining of Everlasting Salvation

adding, less anything vital had been omitted, 'and such like Important Doctrines'.[1] Ian Hazlett has suggested,

> the fact that the Synod of Ulster had to reaffirm this so solemnly indicates a certain degree of dissatisfaction in some quarters of the Church with that Confession, whether of its status or its doctrines. It also reflected growing scepticism about the authority of the church to bind the consciences of its members and impose on them what were perceived as 'human opinions', which seemed, ironically to some, to be a betrayal of the reformation.[2]

---

1 *Records of the General Synod of Ulster, 1691–1820* [Hereafter *RGSU*] i, p. 526.
2 Ian Hazlett, 'Religious Subversive or model Christian?', in D. Smyth (ed), *Francis Hutcheson* a supplement to *Fortnight* 308 (August, 1992) p. 18.

And that was indeed the situation. Not only were 'the great and fundamental Truths of Christianity, according to the Westminster Confession of Faith and Catechisms' being neglected by some ministers of the Synod, but there were those who taught a different doctrine and questioned the right of the Synod to interfere with their conscientious convictions.

It would have been strange if the Irish Presbyterians had remained untouched by the currents of thought which were transforming the theology of the Reformed traditions in Britain and Europe in the seventeenth and eighteenth centuries.

A reaction against the competing dogmatisms which were perceived to have led to the wars of religion of the post-Reformation period, and the new understanding of life and the universe resulting from the scientific movement, combined with an increasing confidence in human reason to put question marks over the methods and conclusions of traditional theologies.

The Dutch theologian Arminius was a pioneer in questioning the axioms of classical Calvinism. Over against the Calvinist emphasis on human impotence and the necessity for divine grace in man's salvation, Arminius had argued that there must be co-operation between divine and human wills: 'The decree of election embraces only those who repent, believe and persevere, and the decree of reprobation applies only to the impenitent'.[3] In response the Synod of Dort of 1618–19 had reaffirmed the five points of Calvinism: Total Depravity, Unconditional Election, a limited Atonement and the perseverance of the Elect.

In seventeenth-century Britain Arminian doctrine was identified with Laudian high Anglo-Catholicism and Stuart autocracy. Therefore this doctrine suffered accordingly as a result of the conflict between king and parliament. One of the by products of the struggle was the Westminster Assembly of Divines and their formulations which became definitive statements of Calvinist orthodoxy for the English-speaking world. Perhaps inevitably the Restoration of the king and Anglicanism in 1660 began in turn the eclipse of Calvinism which was suspect because of its associations with rebellion, civil war and Cromwellian military dictatorship. 'Seldom has a reversal of fortune been so complete', observed G.R. Cragg in his suggestively named *From Puritanism to the Age of Reason*, 'within fifty years Calvinism in England fell from a position of immense authority to obscurity and insignificance'.[4]

Although the national church in Scotland, Presbyterian after 1690, remained officially and legally committed to the Westminster doctrines, a recent survey of theological teaching in the university of Glasgow has judged that 'Older verities were waning as the Enlightenment began to seep through and

3 J.T. McNeill, *The History and Character of Calvinism* (New York, 1954) p. 264.
4 G.R. Cragg, *From Puritanism to the Age of Reason* (Cambridge, 1950), p. 30.

weaken the dogmatic scaffolding'.[5] External conformity co-existed with private and occasionally publicly expressed doubts. John Simson, Ulsterman Francis Hutcheson and William Leechman have been identified as 'the unapostolic succession' who led the advance of the latitudinarians or moderates as they was called in Scotland.[6]

Ulster Presbyterian ministers were normally educated in Scotland, of course, while some, like Samuel Haliday, one of John Abernethy's circle, studied at Leyden in Holland. Abernethy was the son of a Scot, also John Abernethy, who had come over to minister in Ireland. Ejected from the parish of Aghaloo in county Tyrone in 1661 he had ministered for a time to the Presbyterian congregation of Brigh, in the same county, before being installed in Moneymore in 1684. He was moderator of Synod in 1689, the year in which Ireland was convulsed by the conflict between James II and William III for the throne of these islands. Abernethy senior, with Patrick Adair, historian of the beginning of Presbyterians in Ireland, went to England to lobby William when the situation in Ulster deteriorated and Mrs. Abernethy was forced to seek refuge for herself and her children in Londonderry. John, junior, was away from home, visiting relatives in Ballymena who took him with them to Scotland. This may have saved his life for the other members of his family, though not his mother, were casualties of the siege of Derry.

After the Williamite War his father moved to Coleraine and John rejoined the family briefly before entering Glasgow University as a thirteen year old student. In Glasgow he was a contemporary of John Simson, later professor of theology and one of the 'unapostolic succession', who was ultimately restrained from teaching by the General Assembly of the Church of Scotland, though not removed from his chair. As early as 1717 he was warned by the Assembly 'not to attribute too much to natural reason and the power of corrupt nature to the disparagement of revelation and efficacious free grace'.[7] His final indictment enumerated an impressive list of errors—'Arminianism, Unitarianism, Jesuiticalism, Arianism, rationalism, denial of original sin as well as an accusation of belief that the moon might be inhabited'![8] Abernethy subsequently moved to Edinburgh for his theological studies. Dr. Godfrey Brown, in his biographical portrait of Abernethy, claims that George Campbell, Abernethy's theological professor in Edinburgh, was a sound Calvinist, but R.B. Barlow in an article on the career of Abernethy in the *Harvard Theologi-*

5 Ian Hazlett, 'Ebbs and Flows of Theology in Glasgow, 1451–1843' in W.I.P. Hazlett (ed), *Traditions of Theology in Glasgow 1450–1990* (Edinburgh, 1993) p. 15.
6 J. Macleod, *Scottish Theology in relation to Church History since the Reformation* (Edinburgh, 1946), p. 208.
7 J.H.S. Burleigh, *A Church History of Scotland* (Oxford, 1960), p. 288.
8 Hazlett, *Traditions of Theology in Glasgow*, p. 16.

cal Review contends that not enough is known about the content of his teaching because he published nothing.[9]

When Abernethy returned to Ireland he spent some time in Dublin where he was caught up in the excitement surrounding the case of Thomas Emlyn. Emlyn, who was colleague of the Revd Joseph Boyse in the fashionable Wood Street congregation, was found guilty of blasphemy because of his anti-trinitarian opinions and was fined and imprisoned. It is an indication of the talents of the young and inexperienced Abernethy, licensed by the Route presbytery on 3 March 1702, that he should have been invited to succeed Emlyn as Boyse's colleague in Wood Street. Concurrently he was also asked to follow his father as minister of the Coleraine congregation. The congregation in Antrim was also eager to have his services and the Synod of Ulster decided that that was where he should go and he was installed there on 18 August 1703.

He quickly achieved a reputation as scholar and preacher and in 1717 he was called to minister in the Usher's Quay congregation in Dublin. His Antrim congregation opposed this and one of the reasons they advanced was the success of his ministry to the Irish speaking Roman Catholic community on the shores of nearby Lough Neagh. It may seem strange to find a minister who was to be so closely identified with the liberal wing of Irish Presbyterian Church, prominently involved in outreach to Roman Catholics. Abernethy, however, was not anti-catholic because the Westminster Confession declared that the Pope was anti-Christ, but because he regarded the Roman Catholic Church as a supreme example of ecclesiastical tyranny. In his later *Persecution Contrary to Christianity* he attacked Roman Catholicism for its

> narrow party spirit, extinguishing that generous affection to mankind which is the glory of human nature with the most inveterate rancour against all those who are of different opinions concerning points of religion.[10]

Abernethy's hostility to ecclesiastical authority had been awakened and reinforced by his experience of the authority of presbytery and synod in his own church. He had submitted to the Synod's decision in 1703 that he should go to Antrim and had been relieved when it was decided in 1712 that he should stay there and not accept a call to Londonderry. He was not so happy, however, with the Synod's decision in 1717 that he should go to Usher's Quay in Dublin and he obeyed for only three months before returning to

9 A.W.G. Brown, 'John Abernethy 1680–1740, Scholar and Ecclesiast' in G. O'Brien and P. Roebuck (eds) *Nine Ulster Lives* (Belfast, 1992) p. 128; R.S. Barlow, 'The Career of John Abernethy (1680–1740), Father of NonSubscription in Ireland' in *Harvard Theological Review* (1985), dxxviii, p. 401.

10 John Abernethy, *Persecution Contrary to Christianity* (Dublin, 1735), p. 25.

Antrim in defiance of the Synod which acquiesced in the *fait accompli* but found him to be seriously at fault.[11]

He had been strengthened in his dissatisfaction with ecclesiastical authority by the fact that his opinions were shared by a group of ministers and elders with whom he had been meeting regularly since 1705 for mutual edification, known as the Belfast Society. This group included men who might be described as the leading *avant garde* members of the Synod—James Kirkpatrick, minister of the Second Belfast congregation, Michael Bruce of Holywood, Thomas Nevin of Downpatrick and ruling elders like the prominent Belfast physician, Victor Ferguson, forbear of the contemporary Duchess of York. Later they were joined by Samuel Haliday, when he was called to the First Belfast congregation. James Kirkpatrick tells us that they shared books and ideas, considering such subjects as the scriptural terms of the unity of the Church, the nature and mischief of schism, the rights of conscience and private judgement, the sole dominion of Christ in his kingdom and the nature and effects of excommunication.[12] They offered each other expositions of passages of Holy Scripture and exchanged book reviews. James Duchal, Abernethy's successor as minister in Antrim, and later in Wood Street in Dublin, tells us that it was their aim 'to bring things to the test of reason and scripture without a servile regard to any human authority'.[13]

Francis Hutcheson, the distinguished Ulster born moral philosopher, and another of the 'unapostolic succession' in Glasgow, who was later to be regarded as the personification of the eighteenth-century 'New Light' movement in Presbyterianism, was in Dublin in 1718 and reported on the Irish Presbyterian scene to a friend in Scotland:

> I find by the conversation I have had with some ministers and comrades that there is a perfect Hoadly mania among our younger ministers in the north, and, what is really ridiculous it does not serve them to be of his principles but their pulpits are ringing with them, as if their hearers were all absolute princes going to impose tests and confessions in their several territories.[14]

Hoadly, bishop of Bangor, had preached a controversial sermon on 31 March 1717 attacking high church tories and arguing for the removal of penal legislation against Dissenters. Though basically a plea for latitude and toleration

---

11 *RGSU*, i, pp. 532–3.
12 J. Duchal, *A Sermon on the occasion of the Much Lamented Death of the late Revd. John Abernethy* (Belfast, 1741), pp. 36 ff.
13 Ibid., p. xlvi.
14 J. S. Reid, *History of the Presbyterian Church in Ireland* (3 vols., Belfast, 1867), iii, pp. 115–16.

the sermon expounded a liberal Arminian theology which postulated the rationality and moral responsibility of man. Hutcheson also suggested that the Irish ministers had been influenced by Samuel Clarke's sceptical *Scripture Doctrine of the Trinity*, published in 1712, but it is now generally agreed that the Ulster liberals were Arminians and not Arians or anti-trinitarians.[15] A modern non-subscribing Presbyterian scholar has judged that:

> if there was any doctrinal position characteristic of the group as a whole it was not concerning the Trinity but rather their abandonment of Calvinistic predestination in favour of an Arminian standpoint. The one common theme of their writing was that mankind had the natural reason and ability to seek the mind and will of God, and that they had the gift of free will either to reject this knowledge or to apply it towards their own salvation.[16]

It was this position which John Abernethy was to represent and articulate so persuasively.

On Wednesday, 9 December 1719, John Abernethy, in the context of his disagreements with the Synod over his call to Dublin, read a sermon to the Belfast Society, entitled *Religious Obedience founded on Personal Persuasion*, based on Romans XIV.5, 'Let every man be truly persuaded in his own mind'. Persuasion Abernethy interpreted as 'assent formed upon evidence and attentive reasoning' and he contended that there were two necessary conditions of that persuasion:

> 1. That it be deliberate, for sudden and rash conclusions without duly weighing the reasons upon which they were founded, and what evidence there may be on the opposite side, are the reproach of intelligent natures, such as ours.
> 2. Our persuasion ought to be unprejudiced, free from passion or the influence of any consideration except that which should rationally determine us; that is, in the present case, anything but the pure evidence of the mind and will of God.[17]

And it was by rational inquiry that the mind and will of God could be known. Only the willing obedience of the soul to the light of conscience would please God, not the acceptance of the received opinion of others.

15 Ibid., p. 116.
16 J.W. Nelson, 'The Belfast Presbyterians 1670–1830', PhD thesis, Queen's University, Belfast, 1985 p. 108.
17 John Abernethy, *Religious Obedience founded on Personal Persuasion* (Belfast, 1720), pp. 12–13.

It is scarcely necessary to observe that this challenged both Calvin and the articles of the Westminster Confession which taught a very different theology and anthropology. Calvin had taught and the Westminster Confession confirmed that man, as sinner, was incapable of responding positively to God; only God could rescue man from the miry clay of his sinful nature. Abernethy's anthropology, by contrast, was optimistic and benign; he was much closer to the Council of Trent and Arminius than he was to Calvin or the Westminster Confession.

It was the Revd John Malcolme, the elderly minister of Dunmurry, who articulated the conservative response to Abernethy's sermon in a tract entitled, *Personal Persuasion no foundation for Religious Obedience or Some friendly Reflections on a sermon preached at Belfast, December 9, 1719 by John Abernethy*, published in 1720. In this tract he accused Abernethy and his associates of 'pretending to give New Light to the world by putting personal persuasion in the room of church government'.[18] Thus Abernethy and those who thought like him became known as the party of 'New Light'.

Malcolme himself acknowledged that his somewhat slight work was not an adequate reply to Abernethy and he expressed his hope that 'I may awaken some of my revered brethren to give a more full and learned answer to the same sermon'. But no such answer appeared and it is generally recognised that the conservative or 'Old Light' party in the Synod did not at this time have apologists of the same intellectual calibre as the luminaries of 'New Light'; Abernethy, Kirkpatrick and Haliday. They replied to Malcolme in the name of the Belfast Society under the title, *The Good Old Way or A Vindication of some important Scripture truths, and all who preach them, from the imputation of Novelty*. For them, the articles of the Westminster Confession and the decision of the Synod in 1705 to require subscription to those articles by ordinands were the real novelties.

The controversy which divided the Synod of Ulster in the wake of the publication of Abernethy's sermon centred not so much upon New Light theology as upon the practical issue of subscription to the Westminster Confession. Indeed the Belfast Society had been formed in 1705, the year in which the Synod enacted its subscription requirements. In the last paragraphs of his sermon he had underlined the central theme of the whole address, that the authority of private conscience cannot be subordinated to any ecclesiastical authority and that the Christian should not be required to submit to 'Human Declarations and decisions in any point of faith and duty'.[19] It was

18 J. Malcolme, *Personal Persuasion no foundation for Religious Obedience* (Belfast, 1720); T.H. Witherow, *Historical and Literary Memorials of Presbyterianism in Ireland* (First Series) (Belfast, 1879) pp. 218–19.
19 Abernethy, *Religious Obedience*, pp. 42–3.

always to be the claim of the non-Subscribers, as they were also called, that it was not the content of creeds and confessions of faith which they opposed, but the principle of subscription to man-made doctrinal formulae. Equally, their opponents suspected that it was the doctrines of the Westminster Confession to which the non-Subscribers objected. Ian Hazlett has observed:

> If it was largely members of the Belfast Society who made an issue of subscription to man-made confessions of doctrine as somehow intrinsically alien to authentic Christian tradition, it was because they aspired to avail legitimately of a wider spectrum of theological opinion than any single confession allowed—in particular the Westminster.[20]

It was probably inevitable that the Synod's attempt in 1720 to make subscription acceptable to sensitive consciences by a pacific act allowing candidates to offer their own statements of belief in place of passages in the Confession with which they found difficulty, providing that the presbytery concerned was satisfied with their orthodoxy, failed to solve the problem. Almost immediately, Samuel Haliday, at his installation in the First Belfast congregation on 28 July 1720, refused to subscribe in any form at all, affirming his belief that the Scriptures of the Old and New Testaments constituted,

> the only rule of revealed religion, a sufficient test of orthodoxy or soundness in faith and to settle all the terms of ministerial and Christian communion to which nothing may be added by any synod, assembly or council whatsoever.[21]

Nevertheless the presbytery of Belfast proceeded to install him in the First Belfast congregation.

The Haliday case was discussed at the next meeting of Synod in 1721, when a majority of those present reaffirmed their subscription to the Westminster Confession in terms of the pacific act.[22] Twelve ministers, including Haliday, Kirkpatrick and Abernethy refused, and it was from this time that they were known as non-Subscribers. In 1725 the non-Subscribers were gathered in one presbytery, the presbytery of Antrim, which was expelled from the Synod the following year by a narrow majority in which, significantly, the votes of elders rather than ministers determined the Synod's decision.[23]

This did not solve the problem of subscription in the Synod, however, for many in other presbyteries were unhappy about the practice and, by the end

20 Hazlett, 'Religious Subversive or Model Christian', p. 19.
21 Reid, *History*, iii. p. 130.
22 *RGSU*, ii, p. 11.
23 Reid, *History*, iii. p.209.

of the eighteenth century, as J.M. Barkley's research has shown, 'more than two-thirds of the presbyteries [of the Synod] evaded the law and admitted candidates without requiring from them any formal adherence' to the West-minster Confession.[24] It might appear that New Light and non-Subscription had won among the Irish Presbyterians, but that was not the end of the story.

A majority of the Presbyterian laity, well instructed in the Westminster theology of the Shorter Catechism were unenthusiastic about New Light and non-Subscription. This attitude is vividly illustrated in the well known story about the young Francis Hutcheson preaching in his father's congregation in Armagh in 1719, the year in which he was licensed by the Armagh Presby-tery. A large number of the members of the congregation walked out and an irate elder, meeting Hutcheson *père*, explained:

> Your silly son Frank has fashed a' the congregation for he has been babblin' this hoor about a gude and benevolent God, and that the sauls of the heathen will gang tae heaven if they follow the licht of their ain consciences. Not a word does the daft boy ken, speer nor say aboot the gude, auld comfortable doctrines of election, reprobation, original sin and faith. Hoots, mon, awa' wi' sic a fellow.[25]

Authentic or not, and W.D. Killen, completing Reid's history of the Presby-terian Church in Ireland, comments, 'this story is obviously exaggerated',[26] it illustrates a common reaction in Irish Presbyterian pews when New Light was offered from the pulpit. Incidentally Hutcheson himself disclaimed member-ship in the New Light party, but the ideas in his sermon to which the elder objected were clearly New Light. And very soon congregations were able to hear 'the gude, auld comfortable doctrines of election, reprobation, original sin and faith' from Scottish Seceders and Covenanters in the pulpits of dis-senting Irish Presbyterian meeting houses. The fact that the Seceders were able to plant 141 congregations in Ulster over the next hundred years indi-cates the popularity of their conservative Calvinism with ordinary Ulster Presbyterians. Ninety families left Abernethy's congregation in Antrim, which probably encouraged him to move to Wood Street in Dublin in 1730.[27]

24 J.M. Barkley, *The Westminster Formularies in Irish Presbyterianism* (Belfast 1956), p.15.
25 Reid, History, iii. p. 294n.
26 Ibid.
27 Barlow, 'Career of John Abernethy', p. 410. T.H. Witherow quotes the Revd Joseph Boyse, writing to the Revd Thomas Steward in Bury St. Edmunds, on 1 November 1726: 'Mr. Abernethy himself has malcontents in his own congregation, that have petitioned the General Synod's committee for a new erection'. *Historical and Literary Memorials*, First Series, pp. 86–7. The 'newly erected congregation' was commended for assistance from other congregations by the Synod in 1727. *RGSU*, ii, p. 117.

Godfrey Brown has argued that the New Light non-Subscribers, in spite of their apparent success, 'never really succeeded in convincing the majority of the soundness of their beliefs'.[28] More recently, Ian McBride, in his doctoral thesis in which he examines 'Polite Presbyterianism—The Social and Cultural Context of the New-Light Ascendency', contends that the apparent ascendancy of New Light in the Synod of Ulster in the eighteenth century was misleading and, ultimately, superficial. He has shown 'that the New Light had its base in the wealthier meeting-houses'.[29] When congregations were classified at the end of the century to qualify for a graded scale of *regium donum* payments, of eleven congregations paying a ministerial stipend in excess of £100, only two were Old Light. Of the second category with stipends between £75 and £100 there were 20 urban congregations, half Old Light and half New Light. Of the third and largest category, paying less than £75 and mostly rural, almost all were Old Light.[30] When, after the Second Subscription or Arian controversy in the 1820s, seventeen non-subscribing ministers and congregations left the Synod of Ulster, only one of those congregations, Newtownlimavady, where the Revd William Porter ministered, was west of the Bann.

I have observed elsewhere[31] how New Light theology was peculiarly attractive to the emerging *bourgeois intelligentsia* of eastern Ulster, who, like their counterparts elsewhere in western Europe, were susceptible to Enlightenment influences and were critical of what appeared to be artificial and archaic restrictions upon freedom in business, politics and ideas. A rational form of religion, eschewing mysterious and metaphysical dogma, and emphasising duty and responsible behaviour, in other words, 'polite presbyterianism', was popular among them. In the great final confrontation between Old Light and New Light in the 1820s, the Old Light champion Henry Cooke acknowledged that 'a large proportion of the wealth, respectability and commercial interest of the metropolis of the north' was in New Light hands or supported the New Light party.[32]

In Scotland the ascendancy of the Moderates, corresponding to the New Light party in Ireland, owed much to the system of lay patronage which

28 A.W.G. Brown, 'A Theological Interpretation of the First Subscription Controversy' in J.L.M. Haire (ed), *Challenge and Conflict, Essays in Irish Presbyterian History and Doctrine* (Belfast, 1981), p. 36.
29 Ian McBride, 'Scripture Politics' The Religious Foundations of Presbyterian Radicalism in late Eighteenth–Century Ireland, PhD thesis, University College, London (1994).
30 Public Records Office of Northern Ireland, Castlereagh Papers, D 3030/1009, quoted by Ian McBride, 'Polite Presbyterianism' p. 36.
31 'Controversy and Schism in the Synod of Ulster in the 1820s' in J.L.M. Haire (ed), *Challenge and Conflict*, p. 120.
32 *Belfast Newsletter*, 7 July 1829.

allowed lairds—the Crown and the ruling élites of burghs—to present their nominees to minister in parishes of which they were patrons. There was no lay patronage in the Irish Presbyterian Church, but in 1733 the Synod of Ulster had introduced a qualification to their requirement that, in a ministerial vacancy, the successful candidate must have the support of two-thirds of the qualified voters. Henceforth 'said two-thirds are to be reckoned both from the number, quality and stipend of the congregation'.[33] This 'two-thirds men and money' rule, as it was derisively described by its critics, gave undue influence to the wealthier members of a congregation, who tended to be more sympathetic to New Light candidates than the less affluent members of congregations.[34]

In Scotland, social and political changes in the early nineteenth century contributed to the overthrow of the Moderatist ascendancy in the General Assembly. It has been shown that, 'by the 1820s the Assembly was dominated by a more diversified ruling establishment in the wider secular sense'.[35] The growing influence of Evangelicalism was reflected in an increase in the numbers of Evangelical elders who played a part in challenging lay patronage and bringing about the disruption of the Church of Scotland in 1843.

Similarly in Ulster the Evangelical movement, breathing new life into the Old Light party and drawing the General and Secession Synods closer together in their common concern for evangelical outreach in Ireland and the wider world,[36] created an effective majority in the Synod of Ulster against New Light, which had been discredited to some extent by its perceived associations with the political radicalism of the United Irishmen and the disaster of the 1798 rebellion. Significantly the meeting of the Synod of Ulster which marked the beginning of the end for the New Light party, when the overwhelming majority in the Synod reaffirmed their trinitarian faith, was held in Strabane in 1827. Henry Montgomery's biographer, J.A. Crozier, claimed that in the west of the province the cries of 'no surrender' and 'Down with the Arians' were synonymous and the Revd William Porter, new light clerk of the Synod, alleged that it was his support for Catholic emancipation, rather than his Arianism which was the real reason for the campaign against him and his party.[37]

---

33 *RGSU*, ii. p. 187.
34 D. Stewart, *The Seceders in Ireland* (Belfast, 1950), p. 55.
35 I.F. Maciver, 'The Evangelical Party and the Eldership in the General Assemblies, 1820–43' in *Records of the Scottish Church History Society* (1978).
36 *Missionary Sermons and Speeches Delivered at a Special Meeting of the General Synod of Ulster* (Belfast, 1834). The fact that some at least of the New Light, non-subscribing party, had openly avowed Arian and Anti-Trinitarian opinions made them vulnerable to a change of heresy. J.A. Crozier, *Life of Henry Montgomery* (Belfast, 1875), i, p. 108.
37 R.F. Holmes, *Henry Cooke* (Belfast and Ottawa, 1981) p.48

Even in Belfast and the east of the province industrialisation was assembling a new proletarian population who responded more enthusiastically—if they responded to the claims of religion at all—to the certainties of Evangelical teaching than to the intellectual questions of New Light theology. Henry Montgomery alleged with some justification that Henry Cooke, by 'uniting evangelicalism with Orangeism and the countenance of the aristocracy (as opposed to the bourgeois intelligentsia) with the applause of the multitude ... acquired extraordinary popularity and influence'.[38] Cooke was able to isolate and overwhelm the remaining New Light elite in the Synod, opening up the way for reunion with the Seceders to form a stronger base for evangelical outreach at home and abroad. Irish Presbyterians had reasserted their traditional Calvinism by defeating the challenge of New Light which had appeared to be victorious in the different atmosphere of the eighteenth century.

38 *Irish Unitarian Magazine* (Belfast, 1847), ii, no. 2, p. 360.

A Narrative of the Case of Miles Crowly

KEVIN HERLIHY

On 11 May 1760 the Cork Baptist meeting was rejoicing because a twenty year old Roman Catholic convert named Miles Crowly was baptised 'by his own consent' and 'in a public manner'. His baptism was a great public spectacle attended by a 'number of spectators so great that many of the genteelest sort were obliged to go off for want of room'. Even with so large a crowd the baptism went ahead with 'no interruption' and with 'decency and order'.[1] The minister, the newly appointed John Knight, administered the baptism and preached a sermon using a text from St Paul's letter to the Ephesians.[2] Before the actual baptism Miles read aloud the later part of the document here reproduced. The reason for the fanfare was because Crowly had been trained by the Jesuits; at the Irish College at Poitier, France. Even though he was a son of a poor farmer near Bandon, through the influence of his uncle and a benefaction left to the College by a name-sake, he was well educated.[3]

According to his narrative he began having second thoughts about Roman Catholic dogma when he was introduced to Huguenot polemic and when his personal experiences of Jesuit 'Principles and Conduct' led him to believe that they were 'little more than a mere Fabrick of worldly Policies'. From this postulation Crowly extensively assures his readers that his motivations are pure. Using the rational language of New Light theology he explained that his decision stemmed from his 'reasonable Faculties' as well as 'Knowledge and Truth'. His change of religion was 'not from any mean lucrative Motives'. At the end of his apology he returned to the issue of motive by reassuring his readers that 'Truth is the only Object' and ends the passage with a quote from David's psalm of contrition.[4] At the beginning of the public recantation an attempt was made to restore 'the irreparable Wreck of my blasted Reputation'. Unquestionably Miles was protesting too much.

1 Cork City Baptist Church, Cork Baptist Church Book, p. 59.
2 Ibid., p. 59; Ephesians, 4:15.
3 Cork Baptists mistakenly believed that Crowly had a personal relation that provided funds for his education in France. Cork Baptist Church Book, p. 77. However, in 1730 Jeremiah Crowley, a Roman Catholic merchant from Cork, left an endowment of thirty thousand livres to the Irish Jesuit College of Poitiers. Revd Francis Finegan, SJ, 'The Irish College of Poitiers, 1674–1762' in *Irish Ecclesiastical Record*, fifth series, civ (1965), p. 32.
4 Psalm, 51: 6.

The main reason for this particular method of pleading was due to slanderous stories that were circulating and 'the cavils and innuendoes' of paedobaptist Protestants in Cork who had 'apprehended he had sinister views'. These Protestants, abetted by the gossip, believed that the conversion of any Catholic was to be looked upon with skepticism due to the worldly advantages that might be accrued by such an act. The Baptists believed that in this particular case it was a ridiculous notion because 'of all denominations of Protestants they can afford the least encouragement of a worldly sort to proselytes'.[5] Even so, Miles did experience a considerable augmentation of his worldly means as a result of his public declaration. Soon after his baptism, on 23 May, the Irish Baptist Association met in north Tipperary at the town of Cloughkeating and delegates from the Cork meeting recommended Crowly be subsidised for training to become a Baptist pastor. In August of that year he began receiving quarterly payments of £5 from an education fund set up by the Irish Baptists in Dublin. The publication of *The Narrative*, which was printed in Dublin by one of the trustees of the education fund, Samuel Powell, most likely played a significant part in the decision to grant Crowly the stipend. Certainly the other trustees in Dublin, who had no personal experience of Crowly, were impressed by his learning and wit. The Irish Baptists at that time were on the lookout for a 'popular man', and Miles seemed full of potential. The overjoyed meeting provided him with free accommodation, and no doubt made it possible for him to receive tuition payments of 40 shillings per quarter from at least eight students learning French. Put together his annual income was above that of his pastor.[6]

In this story Crowly explains a number of reasons for his momentous decision, but the reasons given were not really expressed with fullness, limpidity or frankness. After being introduced to the general religious ideas of the Protestants Crowly supposedly mused about their different denominational varieties and came to a confused conclusion. However, this confusion was cleared up by his coming 'into the Company of a serious and judicious Protestant'. For some reason the tract failed to be explicit about his actual choice of denomination. However, the person referred to here was the pastor of the Baptist meeting in Cork, John Knight, but 'judicious' was indubitably not the best appellation for depicting him or his character. He originally encountered the Baptists in June 1759 when he came from England as a ministerial candidate for the *Presbyterian* meeting in Cork. After the Presbyterians rejected his candidacy, because they would not 'dispense him from sprinkling infants', the Baptist wooed him to be their pastor. Knight was not

5 Cork Baptist Church Book, p. 60.
6 The Baptist Union of Ireland, Belfast, Acompt Book of the Fund for the Education of young men for the Ministry, f. 21; Grosvenor Road Baptist Church, Dublin, Register Book of Abraham Wilkinson, f. 32; Cork Baptist Church Book, p. 64.

'averse' to the idea of their call to be pastor, if they could provide him with a 'decent maintenance', but nevertheless returned to England in hope of better prospects there. The parties continued to negotiate through the post. Initially he was offered £50 per annum which was not enough. Eventually, in November, he was able to extract £60 per annum, £20 'English money' for travel expenses, advance money of eight guineas to join the Second Annuity Society, along with continuing payment of the annual membership charge of 40 shillings. Subscribing to the Annuity Society ensured his wife of an income of £30 per annum in the event of widowhood. Furthermore he was assured that the congregation spent from £120 to £130 per annum for the support of the ministry and that when their sixty-year-old pastor, Ebenezar Gibbons, expired he would take his place. He arrived in Cork, via Dublin, shortly thereafter.[7]

Crowly's use of references from the Bible had a design as well. The three Latin quotes on the title page were surely designed to bolster Crowly's claim. The first quote, from Proverbs, 23: 23 (not 25), exclaims, 'Buy the truth and don't sell it'. The following two texts are from the New Testament and place emphasis on reason and rationality. However, it seems very unlikely that Crowly could have known the Bible to the extent with which he seasons his tale. After all Knight, who had introduced him to the New Testament, never mind the Old Testament, had only arrived in January. Before meeting Knight, Crowly 'had not been very conversant with that Collection of sacred and inspired writings'. The pastor who was a wily and ambitious man certainly coached Crowly about what to declare. Having an inside view of the thoughts of their quarry Knight was able to make sure that his declaration produced the proper feelings that were desired by the benefactors. After this episode Knight's popularity rose, so that 'many of the Church of England as well as the Presbyterians' attended worship at the Cork Baptist meeting house. Overall the Cork Baptists were extremely satisfied with the accomplishments of their new pastor. Everything seemed to be going so well. Perhaps too well.

It was not long before this bubble of joy burst. Shortly after his joining the Baptists Crowly pledged himself in security for a loan of £10 to one of his relations. At the appointed time the debt was not paid and the creditor had him put in prison. Furthermore, it became evident that Crowly was also in debt for 'at least twenty pounds'. He managed to escape the consequences by enlisting in the army. By 19 April 1761 he had left Cork and was with his regiment at Kilkenny. The meeting did not record 'the worst of his conduct', but did record a warning to 'be cautious of popish converts, especially those bred at colleges, be more wary still of young Jesuits'. The incident confirmed the fears which were already present in the other Protestants who had warned

---

7   Cork Baptist Church Book, pp. 57–8, 324–8.

the Baptists. Although Crowly was clear of the repercussions of his behaviour Knight was not so fortunate.

It is not certain whether or not Knight fabricated this whole incident with Crowly to increase his stature in the community, but it is very likely that he did. He was definitely aware of Crowly's malfeasance for at least three months before the scandal broke. When Crowly was awarded the benefit of the education fund Knight insisted that the money be sent to him directly which the Baptists in hindsight thought peculiar. He was accused of the 'vilest prostitution of the Education Fund', and of 'supporting Crowly in his excesses'. Earlier that year, due to the pressure of the situation, the two of them fell out which led to accusations, made by Crowly, that led to Knight's dismissal. His popularity had been decidedly changed. Knight, who the meeting claimed was 'so remarkable for prevarication', used all of his skill and wit to avoid dismissal, but to no avail. His basic defence was that Crowly's accusations were false because he was 'capable of saying or unsaying it again'. By the end of June the Cork Baptists wanted to put this unseemly incident behind them and let the matter drop on the condition that Knight not try to contact Crowly and leave the country quietly. On his way to Dublin, Knight paid a visit to Crowly, who was now 'lying under the doctors hand', in order to get his 'final dispositions'. At this point he was trying to use the Baptist leadership in Dublin to extract a testimonial letter from the Cork meeting. After failing in his quest he returned to England with a forged testimonial. By January 1768 he had become indisposed due to being sent to gaol at Coventry.[8]

This document demonstrates the peril of taking the meaning of certain religious narratives on face value. The experiences depicted in the narrative are extremely dubious and designed to pander to the sensibilities of the reader. It also shows how awkward it was for Protestants in eighteenth-century Ireland, however well-meaning they were, to evangelise Catholics. Due to the artificial economic advantages that had been put in place earlier in the century there was no incentive on the part of Protestants to persuade the rest of their countrymen to join with them. Irish society, like the rest of Europe, was divided by class, and the class structure was represented by and through religion. The Baptists, due to their 'low condition', naively thought they were immune from religious fraud. However, their deep desire to change their condition made them very susceptible to dissimulation. They were much too eager to compete successfully in the marketplace of religious ideas, which was not a free market, leaving the unscrupulous with a wide scope for manipulation. Therefore, before this incident, they were exceptionally vulnerable to anyone familiar with their personal desire for popularity and willing to use the insight for unsavoury ends.

8   Ibid., pp. 68–72, 82.

A

NARRATIVE

OF THE

CASE

OF

MILES CROWLY,

CONTAINING,

His Reasons for quitting the Communion of
the Church of ROME, and embracing the

PROTESTANT RELIGION.

Publifhed by Himself,
For the Conviction and Satisfaction of all impartial
Persons, whether Catholicks or Protestants.
To which is added, His

RECANTATION.

Veritatem compara; ac non vendito. *Pro.* xxiii. 25.
Omnia explorate: quod bonum fuerit retinete. I *Theff.* v. 21.
—Estote autem semper parati, ad refpondendum cuilibet pe-
tenti Rationem ejus spei quae in vobis est, cum mansuetudine
et timore. I Ep. *Pet.* iii. 15.

Dublin:
Printed by S. Powell, in *Crane-lane*,
MDCCLX.

[Price Two-pence]

A
Narrative, &c.

It must appear evident to a considerate Mind, that Religion ought to be accounted every Man's dearest and most important Interest, consequently, that it is the incumbent Duty of all Mankind to exercise their reasonable Faculties, and make use of the Helps they are furnished with, in order to distinguish the true Religion from the false. Without this Christianity had never been embraced by any, nor Truth ever had the Precedency of Error. Without this, the Heathen, Mahometan, and Jew must continue such, and the grossest Mistakes and most palpable Falshoods, be retain'd and reverenc'd as certain and divine Verities.

This is the necessary result of the neglect of a sober, free Enquiry, and therefore so far and as long as this prevails, the progress of Knowledge and Truth must be obstructed, and Ignorance and Error gain ground in the World. Sensible of this, the great Corrupters of Christianity, have most studiously endeavoured, by ecclesiastical Threats, Prohibitions, Penalties, and the infliction of Corporal Punishments, to restrain the Laity from all Examinations into the Nature, Evidence and Tendency of their Religion; left thereby their Corruptions should be discovered, and they miscarry in their evil Designs.

But it being my unspeakable Happiness to be born in an Age and Country in which this natural Right is not barely tolerated, but freely given and encouraged, I most readily and thankfully accept of it, and would use it in the most discreet Manner I am capable of; and to those Ends only which shall appear justifiable to the *Unprejudiced* and *Impartial*, viz. the Information of my Mind and Settlement of my Judgment in the Principles of true Christian Religion; in order to regulate my Temper and Conduct in such a Manner, as to please God, maintain a good Conscience, and hereafter enjoy that happy Immortality, which the Christian Religion promises to all who sincerely believe and obey it.

Influenced, (I trust) by these, and only these Motives and Considerations, in the Change of my religious Sentiments, I think it both necessary and expedient for the Prevention of *evil Surmises, wrong Constructions,* and *false Representations,* to acquaint the World with the Manner of my Conviction, and the Steps I have taken to that End; which I will do with that *Sincerity* and godly *Simplicity,* which the Nature of the Thing itself, and the Character of a Christian demand.

I am sensible Accounts of this Nature, (which frequently have something particular and extraordinary, and which Combat with the Humours, *Interest,* or *Prejudices* of the World) are too subject to uncharitable, censorious Imputations, and are seldom considered with that *Tenderness, Calmness,* and *Impartiality* of Mind, requisite to determine fairly and equitably concerning them; and this single Consideration, were it not a *small Thing to me, to be judged of Man's Judgment:* and were there not others much more preponderating than that, would be sufficient to deter me from this Publication; but as I am prepared for all Events of that Kind, so the only Favour I would ask my Reader is, that he would desire others should judge of *his,* supposing he were in *like Circumstances.*

There are very few I am persuaded into whose Hands this Narrative may come, but what will agree with me is these general Principles, that the change of our Religion being a weighty, serious Business, should not be *lightly, inconsiderately,* or *indeliberately* undertaken, not from any *mean lucrative* Motives, or *worldly sinister* Ends; that we should not *reject* our old Principles in which we have been educated, till we have *carefully* examined them, and are very *fully* and *rationally* convinced that they are *false* and *erroneous,* nor *embrace* new ones, till we have very *solid* and *substantial Proof,* (as much as their Nature will admit of) that they are *right* and *true*. The reasonableness of this is Self-evident, consonant to which, I have conducted myself in the Subject of the following Narrative, to which I now proceed.

I was Born within a few Miles of Bandon, where my Relations now live, particularly my *Uncle, a Priest, who as my Father's Circumstances gave me but a poor patrimonial Prospect, adopted me, and took the greatest Care of my Education, as he intended me for the Church; and after I had read the major Part of the Classicks, finding I was not altogether incapable of receiving Instructions, he sent me to the University of *Poitiers*, in order to be duly qualified for the Mission.

What Prejudices in Matters of Religion, I insensibly imbibed, while under my Uncle's Tuition, 'tis easy for any Person to imagine, who has but an imperfect Idea of the Virulency and rigid Severity those of his Profession are possessed of: His Sentiments were mine, so nothing remained but to capacitate me to defend them in this heretical Country; to which End I was sent to the Jesuits, as the most expert Champions of the Roman Church.

During my Three or Four Years of my Residence in the College, my Mind was wholly engaged in the Study off Grammar, Humanity, and Rhetorick, when for the further Cultivation of it, I was permitted to read History, and having always free Access to the Library, the first Thing I was anxious to go through, was the History of the Church, which then I looked on as an imperfect Edifice, whose Foundation being laid by Christ and his Apostles, was left to his holy Vicars to be embellished, perfected and finished. About this Time I met with Monsieur *Daillon*'s Justification of the Innocence of the French Protestants Religion; and though its Title forbad me the Perusal of it, yet as *Nitimur in Vetitum*, i.e. 'we eagerly desire what is forbidden,' I ventured to open it, and read his Parallel of the *Roman* Catholick, and the Idolater mentioned in the xliv Chapter of *Isaiah*.

What I then read of that Author (not without Prejudice, which now exercised its most prevailing Power over my Mind) joined with the constant Narratives of the several Persecutions the Protestants continually suffered; convinced me that there were some probable Grounds, for accusing the Church of *Rome* with Superstition and Idolatry, and agitated my Mind and confused Reflections, and but too well grounded Scruples. The Intercession of Saints I thought as derogatory to the Honour of Christ, as Transubstantiation was repugnant to Reason; which having imparted to my Confessor, he gave me this short Exhortation; *Praestet fides supplementum sensuum defectui*; i.e. 'let Faith supply the Defects of Sense', which was insufficient to banish my Doubts and Apprehensions, which multiplied daily, as my Reason encreased, and I began to exercise my reflective Powers.

In this Situation I continued until I was seized with a fevere fit of Sickness, of which, when I was tolerably recovered, my Physician told me I could no longer without hazarding my Life, stay in *Poitiers*, on Account of the disagreeableness of its Air, wherefore the Jesuits proposed to send me to *Bordeaux*, which I readily fell in with, and soon went thither.

My own Observations on the Principles and Conduct of the Jesuits, and the Company which I occasionally met in *Bordeaux*, still more and more convinced me, that the

*Since this was sent to the Press, I had the Affliction to be informed of my Uncle's Death.

Romish Church was little more than a mere Fabrick of *worldly Policies*, and *Antichristian Institutions*. These Convictions increasing, and the State of my Health not mending, I embarked for *Ireland*; but *beu quantum mutatus ab illo!* i.e. 'But what a changed Man!'. How different were my Notions of Popery when returning to, than when I went from it, and how contrary my Opinions from what could be expected from one so long under the Influence of Jesuits and Priests, designed for the same Order myself, and educated where the Romish Religion is profess'd in all its Pomp and Splendour.

I had not been long return'd, till my Uncle observ'd with Grief, how insensible and indolent I was to what he called Devotion and Piety; he frequently urg'd me to confess, and I as often discovered my Reluctance to it; the Consequence of which was, an abatement of his Regard to me, which when I perceived, I went to *Bandon*, where I taught *French*, and had a further Opportunity of informing myself of Protestants, and finding them to be divided into many Parties and Persuasions, I was ready to conclude, *Deus non vacat exiguis*; i.e. 'God is not at Leisure to mind the mean Affairs of Mortals', that all Religions were but Chimaeras, and to prevent the least Retrospect, or Reflection, kept Company as much as I could. But the Fear of God, and the sober Education I had enjoy'd, did not permit those dangerous Sentiments to take Root. In vain did I strive to suppress and stifle the Convictions of my Conscience. The Communion of the *Church of Rome*, I could not abide, and the various Sects which compose the Reformation, prejudic'd me against them all; but after a long Conflict, I resolved to buy the chief and only Happiness the rational Nature was designed for; i.e. Peace of Conscience, and go Incognito where I could *Examine*, *Assent* to, and Profess whatever I judged most conformable to divine Revelation.

I Foresaw the numerous Obstacles which would arise from the World, and it's Manners and Customs, and that it was impossible to escape the Charge of Hypocrisy, or Enthusiasm, which is so insupportable and dreadful in this Age; wherein the Virtuous study to conceal their Piety, more than the Immoral, their Vice or Profaneness; but notwithstanding these Difficulties, I determined to prosecute my former Resolutions, to which End, I shortly after settled in *Cork*, where I had not spent many Weeks before I providentially fell into the Company of a serious and judicious Protestant, to whom I communicated the State of my Mind, in Relation to my religious Scruples, and Enquiries; he asked me a few Questions, as what induced me to doubt of the Truth of the Religion I had been educated in? What Branches of Learning I had studied at the University? What Books I had read in Divinity, &c. to all which I gave suitable Answers; upon which he left me with recommending to me in a very serious Manner, a careful Perusal of the Holy Scriptures, an honest impartial Examination of the best Writers on the Subjects controverted betwixt the Roman and Protestant Churches, a sincere and upright Intention in all my religious Persuits, and constant earnest Prayer to God to assist me in every Thing relative to this important Affair.

This advice as I knew it to be just and seasonable, I readily complied with, and have since adhered to it in the subsequent Course of my Examinations. I then attentively read thro' the New Testament (for 'till now I had not been very conversant with that Collection of sacred and inspired Writings) together with Archbishop *Tillotson*'s Rule of Faith, Mr. *Chillingworth*'s Religion of Protestants, and some other Books, which that Gentleman furnished me with. By these, I was fully convinced, that the present Doctrines and Practices of the Roman Church (for the most Part) have not the *least Foundation* in Scripture, are opposite to the Genius and Design of Christianity, *mere novel Inventions*, built upon *secular Motives* and *Reasons of State and Policy, contradictory to the natural Sense of Mankind, and destructive of real Piety and Goodness.*

Convinced of these Things, and that the Holy Scriptures alone are a sufficient and perfect Rule of Faith and Practice, I now determine by their Evidence (making Use of every Help and Assistance afforded me) to judge of the Truth or Falshood of the Constitution, Principles, Doctrines, and religious Practices of the several Denominations of Protestant Churches, and in Consequence thereof, to become a Member of that which after the best and most impartial Examination, shall appear to me to deserve the Preference in all the fore-mentioned Respects.

As I do not apprehend that the Church has any infallible unerring Head and Guide besides Christ himself, so I am fully persuaded that the Sense and Meaning of Scripture, the sure Rule of Faith, is left to the unprejudiced Judgment of every Individual, which is the Law of Humanity as well as Christianity, from which Law no other Inconveniencies arise than what are inseparable from Human Nature, and on the Whole, not so great as the Evils springing from that total Suppression of Liberty, which occasions the almost invincible Ignorance, and insuperable Prejudices of the Members of the Roman Church, (especially of the Laity) who in that View are the Objects of my sincerest Compassion, and my constant earnest Prayers. May the eternal Father of Light and Love, hasten the Deliverance of this corrupted Part of the Christian World, from the Darkness and Slavery under which they Labour, bring into the Way of Truth those that err and are deceived; and enable all that profess the Christian Religion to keep the Unity of the Spirit in the Bond of Peace, and maintain a right Faith, with a pure Conscience and a holy Life.

This tho' brief, is a very just Account of my past Life, and the Manner of my Conversion from Popery, which if it may in any Measure contribute towards the Satisfaction of any, respecting my Sincerity, or the Interest of true Religion and Piety; it will answer the Design of a Well-wisher to Mankind. I am sensible of my Relations concern for me, and I can assure them I feel the same for them, tho' springing from a different Source; my Respect and Tenderness towards them are not in the least diminished for not coinciding with them in Opinion. I still look upon them as appointed by God, to teach me the Sentiments and Practices of my younger Years, but as they have no just Claim to Infallibility, consequently they have no Pretence or legal Sovereignty to sway my Judgment, determine Truths, or make Articles of Faith for me, and impose them upon my Understanding, for to believe in all Things as our Predecessors did, would be the readiest Way to lay an eternal Bar against the Improvement of our Reason and Happiness. Convinced of this, and that I was to give an Account of myself to God, being able to judge for myself, I did not think it an indispensable Duty upon me to swallow their Opinions without examining what Truth or Falshood there was in them, and measuring them by the only Rule of Determination in Matters of Religion.

I have weighed then and examined their Opinions, with an humble Deference to their superior Character, and would give them the Preference in Matters dubious or of less Moment than my temporal and eternal Welfare; nor did I depart from their Practices, until Reason and Conscience made it necessary, and in the pursuit of my Enquiries, concerning Protestantism, God is my Witness, Truth is the only Object I am in quest of, *no Motives* which might prevent my finding it, *no wrong Considerations of secular Interests or worldly Advantages* shall biass, or determine my Mind for, or against any Church whatsoever; all that I propose, is the *Honour of God*, and the *Salvation of my Soul*, which will bear the Examination of the *last Day*, when all other Inducements will meet with the severest Censure from him, *who requireth Truth in the inward Parts.*[†]

†I would like to thank Dr Thomas P. Power for bringing this document to my attention.

Index